captive bodies
american women writers redefine pregnancy and childbirth

MARY RUTH MAROTTE

Mary Ruth Marotte

captive bodies
american women writers redefine pregnancy and childbirth

MARY RUTH MAROTTE

DEMETER

DEMETER PRESS, TORONTO, CANADA

Published by:
Demeter Press
726 Atkinson College, York University
4700 Keele Street
Toronto, Ontario M3J 1P3
Telephone: (416) 736-2100 x 60366
Email: arm@yorku.ca Web site: www.yorku.ca/arm

Demeter Press logo based on Skulptur "Demeter" by Maria-Luise Bodirsky <www.keramik-atelier.bodirsky.edu>

Cover Art: Judith Kuegler Webster, "The Journey," encaustic on clay board, 6" by 8", 2007. <www.judithkuegler.com>

Cover Design/Interior Design: Luciana Ricciutelli
Printed and Bound in Canada

Library and Archives Canada Cataloguing in Publication

Marotte, Mary Ruth, 1972-
 Captive Bodies : American women writers redefine pregnancy and childbirth / Mary Ruth Marotte

Includes bibliograhic references
ISBN 978-1-55014-999-9

1. American fiction – Women authors – History and criticism.
2. Pregnancy in literature. 3. Childbirth in literature. 4. Women authors, American – Biography. 5. Pregnant women – United States – Biography.
6. American fiction – 20th century – History and criticism. 7. American fiction – 19th century – History and criticism. I. Title.

PS151.M36 2008   813'.509354   C2008-905724-4

To my family

TABLE OF CONTENTS

ACKNOWLEDGEMENTS

There are a number of people to thank for seeing this book to completion. Thank you to Dr. Mary E. Papke, who was excited about and supportive of this project from its inception. Thank you to Dr. Stanton B. Garner not only for imparting his substantial gifts as a teacher and a scholar but also for his humanity and guidance during each of my years as a graduate student. Most importantly, I must thank my family members whose unwavering love and support are the reasons that I began a study of literature. A special thanks to my mother and father, Mary Louise and Michael F. Wilson, who encouraged my love of reading through frequent library visits and wide travel and who continue to enable me through their beautiful care of my children to be both a working woman and a mother. Thanks to my brother, Michael W. Wilson, for always being a protective and proud brother whose own achievements inspired me to attempt seemingly unattainable goals, and to my sister-in-law, Natalie Zimmerman, for the valuable suggestions that she offered at various stages of my writing. I also want to thank my late grandmother, Helen B. Wilson, for inspiring in me a tenacity that comes from enduring trying times. A special thanks, as well, to Dr. Andrea O'Reilly, for seeing the potential in this project.

Finally, I dedicate this book to my husband, Jeffrey B. Marotte, M.D. and our children, Olivia, Ethan, and Simon. They are the very reasons for being.

INTRODUCTION

CAPTIVE BODIES: AMERICAN WOMEN WRITERS REDEFINE PREGNANCY AND CHILDBIRTH

I do not breed well in captivity.

—Gloria Steinem[1]

The last fifteen years have borne witness to a burgeoning of images of pregnancy in popular culture with the emergence of several contemporary texts and Internet sites that treat the subject realistically and often graphically. It is an understatement to say that this has not always been the case. The publication of Kate Chopin's *The Awakening* in 1899 was a turning point, marking the beginning of serious literary contemplation of how the pregnant condition has affected and continues to affect women's participation in both social and intellectual endeavors. Since the publication of Chopin's novel, American women writers, in contrast to their male counterparts, have often defied the notion of pregnancy as idyllic experience. This book will analyze how images of pregnancy differ according to both the subject position of the writer and the discourse employed. In order to offer this analysis, I will consider multiple works from the late nineteenth and twentieth centuries in fiction and in the autobiographical memoir written by American women.

By analyzing certain qualities of historical female captivity narratives, I suggest here that images of pregnancy in literature portray the condition as a type of captivity. My analysis of the pregnant body attempts a more figurative discussion of what may or may not be literal restraint. While classifying the pregnant condition as a state of captivity may connote a negative evaluation, I underscore how these writers have envisioned the condition of captivity as one in which the pregnant woman can realize, perhaps even find power in, a challenging and disturbing loss of subjectivity. Therefore, I explore the use of the term "captive," locating in it a multivalent meaning. To be captive in pregnancy is to reach a kind of sublime, a rapturous experience that has both negative and positive effects on the experiencing subject. In working with various American writers and their valuable studies of this condition, I reveal a genre of "pregnancy literature" that will validate this subject as one worthy of continued intellectual study and critical attention.

Images of pregnancy in literature by women writers are evidence of a similar concern that has lasted more than a century. In *The Awakening*, written in 1899, Chopin works against the idea that pregnancy is an essential part of being a woman. Obviously, she is writing in response to an enormous body of literature before her that proposed a more essentialist point of view. Before Chopin, pregnancy is rarely described as a negative experience. To be sure, Emily Bronte illustrates in the Gothic nature of Cathy's death in *Wuthering Heights* how pregnancy is the cause of Cathy's untimely demise. But, for the most part, the experience of pregnancy is skimmed over, as is, for example, Isabel Archer's pregnancy in Henry James's *The Portrait of a Lady*. For years the pregnant body was concealed, encouraged to be hidden behind layers of clothing, or simply shut off altogether from the outside world through a mandated confinement of the expectant woman. The same can be said of how literature has dealt with the pregnant body through the ages. Rarely in early American literature was the topic of pregnancy even broached beyond a mention of it as the experience leading up to the woman's truly important role—motherhood. According to critic Michael Lund, "conception occurred, pregnancy developed, and birth happened more often in the gaps of nineteenth-century literature than in the text itself" (95). Proof that there has indeed been a renewed interest in this transformative experience is evident in women's writings that argue it is an injustice to deny this time of gestation is a transformative and important one. The authors whom I study here recognize this time as one in which a woman is arguably still privileging her own needs while at the same time coming to realize how those needs will be compromised once the child is born. The changes and transformations that take place are not limited to the physical. It is precisely those psychical evolutions, such as the coming awareness of how one's life is about to be transformed, that are the subject of this study. "Being pregnant, harboring another inside the self," argues Tess Cosslett in her *Women Writing Childbirth*, "challenges our usual notions of identity and individuality" (117). So, how can the pregnant woman, as captive, come to terms with her feelings of psychical incarceration in a society that demands she read the experience as always idyllic and beneficially self-sacrificing? The works discussed here are written by American women who approach the pregnant condition independent of the role of motherhood. In their reflections on the cultural constraints that have "written" the experience out of women's subjectivity, they attempt a timely revision; ultimately, they view pregnancy as worthy of serious philosophical study in the ways that it affects a woman's consciousness and her overall power as a human being.

The American woman's relationship to her pregnant body has long been determined by the culture in which she resides. Critic Suzanne Ketler notes, with particular regard to the western woman, how "control over a pregnant woman's actions comes in the more subtle yet persuasive form of information which encourages her to follow culturally acceptable patterns of behavior" (110). For instance, the dominant concerns repeated in popular serials suggest that weight gain, stretch marks, and proper nutrition (for herself and the baby) should be the focus of the pregnant woman's concern. This study will ascertain how these cultural guidelines have impacted the images of pregnancy in literature by American women. American society, like most western cultures, still places the burden of responsibility for the health of the fetus and mother directly on the shoulders of the pregnant woman herself. Incidentally, acceptance of such responsibility may directly contribute to feelings of captivity in the pregnant woman. Even as the media grants a woman the major role in the creation of the healthy baby, "the same information denies her as a subject who may have desires, cravings, failures, and motivations beyond the well-being of her baby" (Ketler 116). Many critics have noted, for instance, the irony of public response towards the supposedly "natural" pregnant body; in fact, Adrienne Rich describes in her book, *Of Woman Born*, being *uninvited* to speak at a boy's preparatory school in the 1950s when the dean learns of her pregnancy, certain that the boys were ill-equipped to deal with the sight of her prominent belly. Rich's experience suggests a very American discomfort with the pregnant body, a deep uncertainty as to whether or not we should read it as de-sexualized or hyper-sexualized. Lest we dismiss Rich's experience as an isolated episode of the past, there is also evidence in our very recent history that foregrounds this discomfort. That the 1991 cover of *Vanity Fair* featuring a very pregnant and nude Demi Moore was in many venues wrapped to conceal the photo suggests a very real apprehension with regard to reading the pregnant body in the 1990s and today. The cover of the April 2003 issue of *Vogue*, displaying an earth-motherly photo of pregnant Brooke Shields does signal a positive turn from the usual concealment of pregnant bodies in American magazines, but this came close on the heels of a troubling February 2003 issue of *People* magazine devoted to before and after shots of pregnant and post-partum celebrities, clearly delineating the difference between pregnant bodies as fat and unattractive and post-partum speed in returning to the svelte "before" shape.[2] Recent studies show that we are in a similarly dichotomous place in which the pregnant body can be inserted boldly into popular culture as is the case with the newly-retired *Alias* character Sydney Bristow and simultaneously be exploited thoughtlessly in the October 2005 issue of *Elle* with Britney Spears on the cover. While the creator of *Alias* attempted to equate pregnancy and power,[3] the photo spread of and interview with Spears only serve to exploit her fame, (attempt to) re-fashion her image, and, sadly, only emphasize her apparent lack of any self-reflection with regard to pregnancy.[4] The most recent photographs of Ms. Spears in Harper's *Bazaar* (August 2006) offer more suggestive presentations of the maternal form. Obviously intending to mimic the famous Demi Moore cover, Spears is similarly posed and similarly clad in extravagant jewels. She speaks in the interview about the "empowerment" that has come with her second pregnancy but also relays how her ample size defies the expectations of her fans and her role as "superstar." She lays bare her body in several photos but within the short one-page interview is quite ambivalent about the choice to do the spread. Spears seems to want to give herself over to the experience as an empowering one but also realizes that there will always be fans who see this as her least interesting performance. Like Jennifer Garner's Sydney Bristow, the fundamental ingredient of Spears' persona is sexuality. While Americans are more accepting of the visual presentation of the pregnant body, undoubtedly it must fit certain parameters. The excessive weight that Spears gained in both of her pregnancies does not fall into the realm of the acceptable. No matter how much she is airbrushed in the photos of the spread, her look has shifted from sexy to maternal, and maternity is decidedly unsexy in our culture. There was no audience for a sexy pregnant spy (Garner's Bristow), so there is little hope for a sexy pregnant celebrity/pop icon.

Pregnancy literature that proves to be the most influential in shaping a woman's perception of her pregnant body now includes popular works like *What to Expect When You're Expecting* (Eisenberg and Murkoff) and a myriad of others that capitalize on the lack of information a woman is likely to receive from her healthcare provider. Most of these books provide only the bare minimum of information about how to cope with the philosophical questions that present themselves in pregnancy. Instead, they are concerned primarily with de-mystifying the physical concerns and thus providing women with a view of their bodies as depersonalized collective conduits. Along with these books, American women are presented with magazines like *FitPregnancy*, an idealistic, advertisement-driven serial that offers advice similar to that of the books, but in addition to that advice, the American woman is taunted with images of celebrities and their compact bellies, all of which is meant make the American woman only more consumer-oriented, determined to buy the outfit that is the most slimming. In the guise of a helpful guide to staying fit and keeping your baby healthy throughout pregnancy, what is really evident in such pregnancy magazines is an obsession with thinness. From cover to cover every pregnant woman featured could be wearing a prosthetic belly; nowhere in sight are less than thin/toned arms and thighs and perfectly chiseled facial features. The message becomes one in which thinness and pregnancy are equitable goals, and if one does not fit this image, then one has a lot of work to do. The pregnant American woman is sorely captive to this obsession with thinness, as she is to similar cultural imperatives. Such an obsession with thinness is a curious erasure of pregnancy, a way to confine its explosive potential. Should not such an explosion of the body in pregnancy be read as a prelude to a similarly explosive awakening of the mind? Valuable philosophical concerns are completely ignored when the focus is merely on confinement of the body during pregnancy. We can, however, locate evidence that American women have tried and continue to read pregnancy as a transformative experience, even if it is a challenging one in many ways.

Perhaps some view the advancement of technology as another roadblock in establishing pregnancy as a vehicle for thoughtful inquiry. After all, pregnancy becomes so clinical, so predictably laid out month to month, that the mystery of it all is lost in ultrasounds, non-stress tests, and fetal heart monitoring. Although the publication of *The American Way of Birth* (Mitford) and other such treatises written about the problems with women's healthcare in the United States ignited a questioning of reproductive care among a small circle, the great majority of pregnant women in America adhere to the dictates of the medical establishment, unaware of any form of alternative care. I argue that the emergence of doulas, trained midwives, and others who trust women to read correctly the transformations of their own bodies will aid in lessening the feelings of captivity women might experience during pregnancy. Clearly this century has been a monumental one for women given the advances made in prenatal and postnatal care, and to minimize the impact that these advances have had on the birthing female would be wrong. Without a doubt, pregnancy today is a much safer business. Whereas women formerly spent four and a half years pregnant, had their last child at forty, and were expected to live only another twenty years, today a woman spends on average eighteen months pregnant, has her last child by thirty, and is expected to live another fifty years. These statistics bear witness to the positive strides activists such as Margaret Sanger made towards more accessible and safer birth control and abortions. Pregnancy has also become less a biological consequence and more an option, yet the reality remains that while options have broadened, there are still those who seek to limit a woman's control over her reproductive abilities. It is indisputable that for long women have been held captive and conditioned by the religious and the trained medical establishment, especially so through certain medical mandates and accepted protocols regarding the pregnant condition.

A feminism grounded in women's bodies is a complicated venture, to say the least, and this is undoubtedly why many feminists have derided a study of the maternal body as reductive and essentialist. The introductory chapter of a feminist reader entitled *Writing on the Body: Female Embodiment and Feminist Theory* (Conboy, Medina and Stanbury) fails even to reference the pregnant and birthing body except to refer to it as a sort of "entrapment" that places restraints on a woman's productivity and circumscribes her movements. Anorexia, even menstruation and menopause are considered, but to write about pregnancy and childbirth is to be anchored, it seems, so closely to a historically inscribed female body that many shy away from any association at all with what they see as an essentialist enterprise. Elizabeth Grosz tries to sort out this hesitancy within feminist discourse to approach the pregnant and birthing bodies in her *Volatile Bodies*:

> Where patriarchs have used a fixed concept of the body to contain women, it is understandable that feminists would resist such conceptions and attempt to define themselves in non- or extracorporeal terms, seeking an equality on intellectual and conceptual grounds or in terms of an abstract universalism or humanism. (14)

In her summarization of the different feminist schools of thought, Grosz explains the perspectives of the egalitarian feminists (Simone de Beauvoir, Shulasmith Firestone, and Mary Wollstonecraft are a few) as distrustful of maternity and a focus on the body that they view as limiting a sense of equality and philosophical transcendence. While Grosz gives credence to the egalitarian perspective, she also recognizes a new school of theorists that have emerged (Luce Irigaray, Hélène Cixous, Gayatri Spivak, Judith Butler, Monique Wittig) who argue, as Grosz notes, that "the body is crucial to understanding woman's psychical and social existence" (18); furthermore, this body (and the pregnant and birthing body should be acknowledged as occupying such a position) "is neither brute nor passive but is interwoven with and constitutive of systems of meaning, signification, and representation" (18). Grosz furthermore argues that the female body is not something to be overcome; instead, it is a crucial "site of contestation" and will be treated as such in this study of the maternal body.

Perhaps because of these medical advances and perhaps also in spite of them, the pregnant body has become in the twentieth and twenty-first centuries a more high-profile topic for written discussion in both high and popular literature. As mentioned before, the famously popular *What to Expect When You're Expecting* (Eisenberg and Murkoff) has become a virtual Bible for pregnant women in the United States. But even as a discussion of pregnancy has entered the mainstream, there is still very little inquiry beyond the practical wisdom found in the pages of such self-help guides. Apparent in Naomi Wolf's *Misconceptions* is an awareness regarding this lack of philosophical questioning of pregnancy and a determination to undermine a set of beliefs about pregnancy and childbirth that have permeated American culture for years. Yet Wolf is not the first to attempt such an alternate discussion. One might look, for instance, at Barbara Ehrenreich's and Dierdre English's *For Her Own Good*, published in 1978, and the growing body of bio-ethical discussions of pregnancy by contemporary (usually women) philosophers. Ehrenreich and English anticipate many of the concerns that women are facing today such as how much of a role the medical establishment should have with regard to pregnant bodies. Likewise, in her chapter entitled "Pregnant Embodiment: Subjectivity and Alienation" from her *Throwing Like a Girl and Other Essays*, philosopher Iris Marion Young notes the oftentimes conflicting emotions she experiences in her pregnant state. She challenges the notion that there are two forms of experiencing the body—as subject and as object—and argues that pregnancy "provides a radical challenge... to this dualism" (163) given that the subjective and objective become temporarily blurred. Young also asserts that the actual birthing process generates "extreme suspension of the bodily distinction between inner and outer" (163) and challenges as well the phenomenological understanding that her awareness of her body in its pregnant form, "the massiveness, the lost balance," only serves to alienate her from her body, imprisoning her within the experience (164). Young argues that she is not merely a captive to her body's transformative process but also an actor fully invested in what she sees as a performance in which "certainly there are occasions when I experience my body only as resistance, only as a painful otherness preventing me from accomplishing my goals. It is inappropriate, however, to tie such a negative meaning to all experience of being brought to awareness of the body in its weight and materiality" (164).

Pregnancy is, as Julia Kristeva writes in "Women's Time," "a dramatic ordeal: a splitting of the body, the division and coexistence of self and other, of nature and awareness, of physiology and speech" (364). Kristeva rightly questions Sigmund Freud's argument that to desire pregnancy is to desire a replacement for the absent phallus, and she is clear in her argument that there is and always will be a desire by the majority of women to experience pregnancy. Kristeva thus affirms both the experiences of pregnancy and motherhood as creative acts and wonders at the fact that we have previously not been able to imagine them as such. Robin May Schott, in her article entitled "Resurrecting Embodiment," expresses a desire to return to a more material approach to treating pregnant and birthing bodies. She does so not to reduce a woman to the physical but to explore how a body houses rich and unexplored truths. In Schott's opinion radical feminists who refuse to discuss pregnant bodies and postmodern feminists who deconstruct "women" "reiterate a conception of reason drawn from ascetic philosophy from Plato to Kant" (172), inhibiting a productive discourse that makes room for pregnancy as a topic worthy of philosophical consideration. Schott seeks to explore an alternative to this ascetic tradition that can "help develop 'women'-defined images and practices of pregnancy and childbirth" (172). After all, as Schott explains, in rejecting pregnancy and childbirth, "we reject the experience of pregnancy as a source of knowledge and empowerment" (173), but she realizes, as does critic Elaine Orr, the rather strategic way that we must treat such a philosophical consideration of pregnancy and childbirth. While pregnancy and childbirth are not her central concerns, Orr, in her *Subject to Negotiation*, proposes a way of reading women's texts that suits the study of maternal bodies. Orr argues that negotiation is critical in approaching certain "demanding sites of feminism and a number of other theoretical schools" (2). Orr speaks of negotiation as a way to compromise without becoming compromised, a way to negotiate without being negotiated. She recognizes the division among feminists—division exists across race, class, and sexuality. What this study seeks to do with the subjects of pregnancy and childbirth is a type of negotiation, in Orr's words, to achieve "[r]ather than a frontal assault on gender, [that we might work] within some of the motifs of gender identification in order to create a space for influencing change" (7).

In the opening lines of "Motherhood According to Giovanni Bellini,"

Kristeva advocates further study of pregnant bodies not by idealizing the condition but by challenging her reader to rethink its philosophical potentialities:

> Cells fuse, split, and proliferate; volumes grow, tissues stretch, and body fluids change rhythm, speeding up or slowing down. Within the body, growing as a graft, indomitable, there is an other. And no one is present, within that simultaneously dual and alien space, to signify what is going on. "It happens, but I'm not there." "I cannot realize it, but it goes on." Motherhood's impossible syllogism. (301)

Kristeva, like Schott, seeks to reaffirm pregnancy and maternity as conditions worthy of considerable attention, arguing that some avant-garde feminist groups reject these experiences wrongly because they "identify motherhood with that idealized misconception [of traditional representations of femininity absorbed by motherhood]," while circumventing "the real experience that fantasy overshadows" ("Stabat Mater" 308). Susan Bordo, in one of her many fearless attempts to tackle the question of the body, reiterates the importance of at least considering pregnancy as a worthy focus of our philosophical and cultural focus in her *Unbearable Weight*, posing the question of whether "the unique configuration of embodiment presented in pregnancy—the having of an other within oneself, simultaneously both part of oneself and separate from oneself" might present "a distinctively female epistemological and ethical resource" (36).

Like Young, Kristeva, Schott, and Bordo, Adrienne Rich's interest in pregnant bodies is multi-layered, driven by both fascination and repulsion, and Rich's work, which pre-dates the other three writers' work, was undoubtedly influential to their theoretical positionings. If one were casually to skim Adrienne Rich's *Of Woman Born*, one might interpret her experience of pregnancy as quite negative since she does categorize the child in her womb as "a foreign body introduced from without: an alien" (64). Moreover, Rich is painfully honest in noting that her pregnancies were physical reminders of the "institution" that allowed her "only certain views, certain expectations" (39). Nevertheless, Rich uses her influential voice not simply to castigate the experience as one that should be avoided; rather, she meets pregnancy head-on, carefully recognizing the power that her pregnant body has on others and on her own personal development. Rich is aware of the striking dualism of her condition. While she is cognizant of the impositions that pregnancy makes on her body and mind, she likewise recognizes the potential power inherent in her condition: "I have come to believe...gestation and fruition of life which can take place in the female body has far more radical implications than we have come to appreciate" (39). Rich's work thus serves as a bold reminder of the complexity of living as a pregnant body. She underscores how "the body has been made so problematic for women that it has often seemed easier to shrug it off and travel as a disembodied spirit" (40), and Rich is not here even directly referring to the *pregnant* body. While Rich describes her own pregnancy as something of an allergic reaction, she does not turn away from a confrontation with it.

Another such writer who confronts pregnancy and motherhood directly is Tillie Olsen, the famous working-class feminist writer and critic. She reminds her readers in *Silences* that "in our century as in the last, until very recently almost all distinguished achievement has come from child-less women" (31). Her list of such writers is intended to sound off an alarm, suggesting that many women writers have been "silenced" by their maternity. Since many female writers consciously avoid maternity, our representations of maternity, and especially pregnancy, are relatively few. Nevertheless, did not the feminist movement of the 1970's in America serve to make pregnancy less a matter of destiny and more a matter of choice, planning, and personal growth? Olsen further explores how there are a growing number of women choosing to combine pregnancy and motherhood with careers in writing and other creative fields. Included in her list are a number of writers whom I will study here, but still there are those who fear that a concentration on one's reproductive abilities would necessarily separate and therefore undermine the goals of feminism, doing so by forcing what is viewed by many feminists as a troublesome distinction between male and female. With that being said, the reality (not to be promoted as the ideal) is that a significant number of women will continue to gestate, so why not study the experience of pregnancy as one possible way to heighten self-understanding, even if it is not the only way to achieve it? Must we read pregnancy wholly as an experience that inhibits female autonomy? To read pregnancy as Simone de Beauvoir does, as a captive state in the most traditionally negative sense, and then to conclude that it should merely be avoided seems limited and limiting; a study of how such captivity furthers our knowledge as human beings is crucial to those who choose to involve themselves in pregnancy and childbirth.

Anthologies such as *This Giving Birth* (Tharp and MacCallum) show that such an investigation of pregnancy and childbirth is underway in literature. The essays included in this anthology do in fact discuss a variety of images of pregnancy in literature, always emphasizing the potential for empowerment available through the experience but presenting as well the sordid, darker side of pregnancy, pregnancy as a result, for instance, of incest and rape. Such an anthology certainly hints at the fact that pregnancy literature is indeed becoming a genre of its own, and their inclusion of more problematic images of pregnancy within literature inspires more thought on this topic. It suggests that both the radical and postmodern evasion of a discussion of pregnancy is unproductive and possibly dangerous in that it can prevent a study of pregnant bodies as a source of knowledge and empowerment. Robin May Schott views this refusal to tackle this issue as a mistrust of embodiment, "which precludes an affirmation of birthing in philosophical thought" (175). Tess Cosslett, in her *Women Writing Childbirth*, observes some of the loaded potential of the pregnant body, how a woman's sense of self can be significantly challenged, how

> a mother can feel in harmony with the foetus inside her, or she can feel it as a hostile antagonist; she can experience birth as a splitting apart of her body, and of her mind from her body, or as a flowing process that integrates body and mind in harmonious co-operation; childbirth can create a new, more solid self for the mother, or it can disperse her sense of identity. (117)

Perhaps it is because of writers like de Beauvoir and others who view pregnancy as a debilitating experience, women simply must endure that I am intrigued with both understanding such a viewpoint and revising it. Pregnancy is certainly captivity, but I am fascinated with how notions of captivity might be reexamined. Throughout this book, then, I will write of pregnancy, as portrayed by the numerous writers I have chosen to study, as a version of captivity. My grounds for such an analysis come from observing how the newly emerged genre of historical female captivity narratives defines the experience of captivity. Captivity, though often simply viewed in the pejorative, paradoxically becomes for these female captives a strangely invigorating experience when they learn to see beyond the restrictions that captivity normally implies; in fact, through their individual reactions to captivity, they are able oftentimes to reclaim a greater sense of agency than they have ever previously experienced. Historical female captivity narratives, Christopher Castiglia notes, provide examples "of female strength, endurance, and even prosperity," revealing texts which "persistently explore generic and cultural changes, divisions, and differences occasioned by the captives' cultural crossings" (4). Early American captivity narratives, specifically those of Mary Rowlandson, Hannah Dustan, Mary Jemison, and Sarah Wakefield (anthologized in Derounian-Stodola 1998) provide us with a definition of captivity that, oddly enough, helps equate the experience of pregnancy to a literal and figurative captivity. Their time in captivity shows the experience as both a denial of female agency and a reclamation of it. For the purposes of relating pregnancy to captivity in this study, I focus on the 1682 publication of the Mary Rowlandson's captivity narrative. Literal captivity, a descriptor that best fits Rowlandson's circumstances, evokes in this woman conflicting emotions. Her experience as a captive is a contrary state in which she experiences both fear and empowerment, both a distancing from community and a recognition of inner fortitude, both apprehension and resolute action. These contraries function to energize her both physically and spiritually so that ultimately she reaches a heightened understanding of self. Acknowledgement of the potential in reconciling—or even merely in experiencing—such contraries is helpful in a discussion of the pregnant condition.

My intention is not to minimize the great pain or hardships that these captive women suffered in their respective circumstances, nor do I wish to minimize the great joy that can be experienced during pregnancy. What is apparent is that through such forced endurance, specifically with regard to pregnancy, one might ultimately transcend the baseness of implied captivity and enjoy the rewards of a body that is captive, essentially becoming aware of the necessary roadblocks on the way towards knowledge and greater enlightenment. Through a close study of what the term "captivity" might begin to encompass in light of Rowlandson's, Dustan's, Jemison's, and Wakefield's narratives, I hope to highlight in the first chapter of this study how the captive pregnant body might be alternately read.

"Captivity" is, indeed, a loaded term. Pregnant bodies are complex captive bodies given that pregnancy illustrates the epitome of a complicated captor/captive relationship. But who exactly is the captor? Essentially in pregnancy the captor is the captive, which makes for a strangely masochistic relationship. At the same time, to be captive to something implies enchantment, to have complete attention beyond rational control. The pregnant woman, one can argue, is in a captivated state: entranced, mesmerized, rapturous. She is neither living purely for herself nor for the being that she is carrying but for both simultaneously; in fact, she must reconcile the care that she gives herself with that for the growing being inside her. The materiality of the belly (and the constricted movement typical of late pregnancy) and the restrictions of that body usually enforced by the healthcare provider are both reminders of captivity. Although captivity is generally read as restrictive, and Americans in particular fear such restriction of bodily movement and spatial mobility, what I assert is that there can be heightened philosophical understanding gained in becoming a captive of, in, and to one's own body. So, the term "captivity" can be expanded to include its many derivatives, including "to be held captive" or "to be captivated."

Contemporary images of pregnancy in literature bear resemblance to historical captivity narratives in showing pregnant bodies to be bodies of resistance, creating essentially a version of captivity, a forced confrontation of limits that sparks potential growth and intense examination. Even in the darkest images of pregnant bodies in literature, we can see a kind of hope in recording and giving voice to the experience. Essentially, a woman goes from being a captive (with all the negativity that the term implies) to reimagining the experience as a rapturous one by becoming completely captivated by it. Each author highlighted here feels the experience to be worthy of consideration, thus demonstrating how necessary it is to pay critical attention to how pregnant bodies have been and will be considered in the future, in both literature and in the social world. While perhaps early literary images of pregnancy often show the condition to be akin to captivity in the most negative sense, perhaps future images will show a reconsideration of such captivity.

Anne Bradstreet, one of America's earliest female writers, did not have the luxury of writing about pregnancy as a social and intellectual concern, for she was too busy trying to survive in a demanding environment, writing her poetry while taking care of her multitude of children. However, there are hints even in her work (in the "gaps," if you will) that she does consider how her pregnancies affect her daily existence. In her poem "Before the Birth of One of Her Children" in which she ostensibly speaks to her husband, she is quite obviously preoccupied with the very real possibility of death in childbirth when she urges him to "look to my little babes, my dear remains./ And if thou love thyself, or loved'st me,/ These O protect from stepdames's injury" (151). Contemporary writers might speak of the figurative death (intellectually, socially) of the mother during and after pregnancy, but with Bradstreet we have a *literal* fear of her own death. In Bradstreet's lifetime, pregnancy was portrayed as duty, no matter how dangerous; even in her own works she attempts to settle all her affairs before this new life emerges, a life which could quite possibly destroy her own.

Such glimpses into the experience of pregnancy are few in American literature, but as we move into the nineteenth century, Harriet Jacobs shows us how she is able to assert a sort of control by becoming pregnant. Though the risks of danger in pregnancy and childbirth were still very real in Jacobs' day, her account of her own pregnancies shows her to be aware of how subjectivity might be won through an understanding of—or at least possession of—one's body. In her autobiographical *Incidents in the Life of a Slave Girl*, Jacobs, a literal captive of her white master, wards off his advances by becoming pregnant by a neighboring landowner. Her pregnancy signifies choice in a life that has offered her very little in the way of options. Therefore, her desperate act wills her pregnant body to become her shield to insure that her children will not be slaves to a dangerous master as she has been. Although her pregnancy forces her to take a defensive position and ultimately forces her into hiding for seven years in the crawl space of her own grandmother's shed, unable to commune with her children at all, she emerges confident that she has chosen the proper path. In studying Jacobs further we see how this reproductive ability, combined with the materiality of her belly, virtually defines Jacobs' entire existence; as Michelle Burnham writes, "she is multiply confined, captive several times over" (148). When she makes the choice to become pregnant, her subjectivity is strangely both revoked and restored.

A text like Jacobs' is rare before the twentieth century. In fact, for centuries, images of pregnancy have been held captive by texts written by men who neither had the interest nor the inclination to include such images in the main frame of the text. Rather, such images were relegated to the margins or the gaps entirely. Women might be highlighted in their mothering/nurturing role, but never was the period of gestation deemed a worthy subject for contemplation or discussion. In the few images of pregnancy found in texts before the twentieth century, it is evident that pregnancy is read through a masculine lens. Henry James, widely considered one of the most important writers of the twentieth century and a contemporary of Chopin, did not choose to include pregnancy in his narratives at all. In both *The Portrait of a Lady* and *The Golden Bowl*, children are conceived, born, and manage to mature a few years or to die in the gaps between chapters. One can only imagine how James's Isabel Archer might have experienced her pregnancy, but James is uninterested in that aspect of the narrative. These omissions are fascinating for the ways that they have shaped women's subsequent writings on pregnancy, for they are often the reason that women have felt compelled to write the pregnancy experience. In an effort to develop the idea that writer Kate Chopin was indeed moving towards the development of a new genre of literature, it is imperative to take a step back to reveal just what Chopin and her twentieth-century followers were reacting to and writing against.

Images of pregnancy written by men differ a great deal from those by female writers, whose expressions on the subject are arguably drawn from a very real philosophical imagining of the pregnant body. In Ernest Hemingway's "Indian Camp," one of his semi-autobiographical "Nick Adams" stories, a Native American woman undergoes a crude caesarean section at the hands of Nick's physician father. That the physician enters the scene and believes himself to be "taking care of" the situation is arrogant and absurd. What Nick learns from his father is only that "[the woman's] screams are not important. I don't hear them because they are not important" (Hemingway 16). His distance from the birthing body is profound, and the Indian woman's voice is overwhelmed by the doctor's own need to feel a sense of power over her body. Moreover, Hemingway does not treat the Indian woman's pregnancy through her own eyes. When her husband is found above his wife on the bunk with his neck cut, an apparent suicide, we see pregnancy and childbirth as overwhelming and potentially a violation of man's ability to control the female body. Finally, there is no utterance from the woman herself; essentially, her child-birthing experience has been as violently yanked from her as the child is from her womb. Clearly this is not a story centrally about pregnancy or childbirth but, rather, the interaction and failed communication between a father and a son; though Hemingway is interested in the ways that communication is affected when pregnant bodies are involved since he tackles it yet again in one of his most popular stories, "Hills Like White Elephants." The transformation that is going on inside Jigg's body necessarily transforms her relationship with her companion, holding them captive and in one place after a series of seemingly unfulfilling adventures. Though conflicted about her apparent pregnancy, Jigg clearly sees potential in her body whereas her companion merely sees unnecessary self-sacrifice. Both Jigg and her companion ignore the "unnamed" problem that is behind their inability to communicate effectively. Jigg is grounded in what is happening to her body only to have her lover dismiss the pregnancy as something to be taken care of by elimination: he wants her empty. Though Hemingway's stories prove suggestive with regard to pregnancy and the birthing body, what we fail to see in these examples is a view from the female point of view with regard to the experience; in these texts, we may see in "Hills" only an issue concerning the pregnant body and abortion or, in "Indian Camp," Nick Adams' physician father's assumed ownership of the Native American woman's birthing body as he performs the necessary surgery to extract the child from her womb.

Later dramatists Tennessee Williams and Edward Albee prefer, when dealing with pregnancy in *A Streetcar Named Desire* and *Who's Afraid of Virginia Woolf*, to use the "pregnancies" in the texts as a means of foregrounding undercurrents of tension and strife. Williams uses the actuality of Stella's pregnancy more as a testament to Stanley's virility than as a way for her to gain legitimate footing within the narrative. Stella's condition does not empower her; rather, it weakens her to both Stanley's will and his physical attacks. While her pregnancy is a determining undercurrent throughout the entire play, we do not see it from her perspective at all. Instead, it is merely a weapon that Stanley wields to dominate both Stella and Blanche. Stanley's control over Stella is heightened in her pregnancy, his claims upon her body made even more explicit. After Stanley strikes Stella for criticizing the card game, she flees upstairs from his wrath. Stanley's reaction to Stella's "abandonment" is to infantilize her further. Her pregnancy allows him to do this when he verbalizes his frustration with her absence by repeatedly screaming that he wants his "baby." Given her pregnant condition, we might interpret his use of language to be either referring to Stella or to the unborn child of whom he is already assuming sole claim. Throughout the text Stanley attempts to assume such control, whether it be his determination not to be cheated out of part of the proceeds from the sale of Belle Reve or to be cheated out of his ownership of Stella's pregnant body, and, therefore, *his* child. Clearly, Stella's pregnant body does not function as a shield to Stanley's angry outbursts, but her one scene of defiance does show her to be capable of criticizing Stanley, even if on the most elemental of levels. Her disappearance "upstairs" shows her physically distancing herself from the imposed captivity of her home, where her pregnant body is seen only as the verification of Stanley's sexual potency. Williams' choice to have Stella pregnant during the play shows him to be interested in how the pregnant body becomes a societal body in many cases. Stella's pregnancy affects profoundly the interactions between herself and Blanche, between Blanche and Stanley, and between Stella and Stanley in that it provides a subtext. Both Blanche and Stanley infantilize Stella, Blanche in her reveries about how splendid and idyllic it would be to have a baby, and Stanley in his further subjugation of his wife. Stella does not become empowered by her pregnancy; if fact, her dependence on Stanley only increases.

In sharp contrast to Williams' work, in Albee's play there is no actual pregnancy, only Honey's "hysterical" one. George and Nick openly discuss Honey's "slim hips" to underscore the fact that she is unable to conceive or bear children. The fact that Honey spends a good deal of time prostrate on the bathroom floor suggests that she possesses certain demons regarding her inability to "swell up" legitimately. Albee nevertheless suggests, through both his portrayal of Honey and of Martha, that pregnancy and motherhood might be a source of comfort in the face of considerable despair. Again, as in earlier texts written by men, the discussion of pregnancy, whether a true pregnancy or a "hysterical" one, is managed only by the male characters. Further, the language that they use to describe pregnancy is euphemistic, suggesting a deep alienation from the female body and its capabilities. To be fair, the fact that these male writers include pregnancy in their writings at all reflects a legitimate interest in the condition, but ultimately these texts are unsatisfying to those who view pregnancy as a useful topic of study.

We need only look back to the year 1899, specifically to *The Awakening* with its confrontation of the legitimate restraints and literal fears surrounding pregnancy and childbirth, to find satisfaction. Chopin's novel is a monumental portrayal of how pregnancy and childbirth potentially limit the scope of the women in the Louisiana Creole society of which she writes. Before Chopin breaks new ground with *The Awakening*, images of pregnancy and childbirth were, as Michael Lund points out, "constricted by narrative strategies reflecting specific social codes that governed the understanding and recognition of human reproduction, the conventions of betrothal, marriage, and adultery, and beliefs about identity, heredity, the material and the spiritual" (95). In her own short story "Athénaïse," Chopin describes the protagonist as feeling an "heir to some magnificent inheritance" (412) during pregnancy, "her whole passionate nature aroused as if by a miracle" (411). Patricia Hopkins Lattin argues, however, that even in the earlier short stories "Desiree's Baby" and "Athénaïse," Chopin's illustration of pregnancy is more complicated than it might seem on the surface. For instance, Lattin observes that "during their pregnancies both Desiree and Zoraide see childbirth to represent hope; however, in both cases the hope and the beauty of childbirth are destroyed by the tyrannical systems which originally caused the women's unhappiness: slavery in one case and male-domination colored by the results of slavery in the other" (9). Chopin moves on to an even more ambitious representation of pregnancy and childbirth with *The Awakening*. Adèle Ratignolle, the "mother-woman" of Chopin's story, is pregnant for the duration of the text and is the focus of a particularly vivid childbirthing scene in which Edna Pontellier plays a significant part. That Chopin has Adèle attempting to persuade Edna of the merits of pregnancy and childbirth within the text (and not between the lines) is transgressive for the time of publication in that while Adèle speaks the appropriate words for the times, Chopin's descriptions of her painful physical experience and subtle desperation qualify the impact of her pleas for Edna to honor her motherly duties. Moreover, Edna's reaction to Adèle's insistence on her witnessing the birth fly in the face of all that is then acceptable behavior for women. Indeed, Adèle's failure to bring Edna "back into the fold" of maternal beings allows Edna to elude the captivity she formerly endured with the carrying and birthing of her own children. Further, *The Awakening* suggests the burgeoning influence of the medical establishment in Chopin's portrayal of Edna's "sleeping" through her pregnancies.

After Chopin takes her transgressive leap, the genre of pregnancy literature, if one can call it such, experiences a significant boom, and the majority of writers who deal with the subject portray the experience as akin to a sort of literal and figurative captivity, writing of the condition openly and fearlessly. In addition to an analysis of *The Awakening*, I devote the second chapter to women writers whom we now look back on as some of the defining female voices of the twentieth century. Alongside Chopin, I study the common interest in pregnant bodies found in Charlotte Perkins Gilman's *Herland*, Edith Wharton's *Twilight Sleep*, and Flannery O'Connor's "A Stroke of Good Fortune." Critic Michael Lund argues that Charlotte Perkins Gilman's novel *Herland*, published in 1915, follows the ideas of Chopin by including a narrative in which "conception and birth were at least substantially, if not wholly, present in the body of the text rather than being relegated to its gaps and pauses" (111). Although she is dealing mainly with an upper-class perspective, Edith Wharton explores in her novel *Twilight Sleep* issues of autonomy with respect to pregnant and birthing bodies. Her work inspires considerable thought as to whether or not drug therapies during childbirth enhance or detract from a woman's subjective experience. Wharton illustrates this issue in her novel through a sincere questioning of the intent of the medical establishment with regard to pain management in pregnancy, and she proposes that numbing the body may be a way to inhibit a woman's full involvement in what might be a very transformative experience.

Another writer who is united with Chopin, Gilman, and Wharton in her dedication to bringing women's bodies into literary discourse is the great Flannery O'Connor. Her short story "A Stroke of Good Fortune," is a pivotal piece that depicts pregnancy as anything but good fortune. In fact, her protagonist, Ruby Hill, is in complete denial that pregnancy is even a possibility. When she is forced to accept the truth, as Claire

Kahane argues, her "literal pregnancy becomes a Gothic horror imprisoning [her] in a biological identity with her mother which is perceived
as tantamount to death" (245). The most profound difference between
the working-class perspective and that of O'Connor is that O'Connor
presents Ruby Hill as less concerned about the financial obligations
that her pregnancy presents than she is the psychological ramifications
of her condition. Ruby feels a keen repugnance towards her body, and
she views the life growing inside her as vampiric, "waiting to make his
mother, only thirty-four, into an old woman" (O'Connor 52). Essentially,
O'Connor provides in the pregnancy genre a notable "turn" from issues
of literal captivity to issues of psychological captivity. Such a dramatically negative reading of the pregnant body could certainly not have been
done and read by such a large base of readers if Chopin had not taken
the first step towards a realistic interpretation, for which step she was
crucified, at least in the literary sense. Although it is impossible to prove
that O'Connor was directly influenced by Chopin's *The Awakening*, it is
obvious given O'Connor's bold treatment of Ruby's pregnancy that Chopin
at the very least caused a rupture in pregnancy discourse, enough so that
later writers have felt comfortable treating the subject more candidly.
As Julie Tharp and Susan MacCallum-Whitcomb note in their introduction to their collection of essays entitled *This Giving Birth*, Chopin "did
serve as a midwife of sorts, for her efforts enabled later writers to bring
their own creative work to term" (4). Indeed, Chopin inaugurates what
we might label a "pregnancy genre" with her creation of the enigmatic
Edna Pontellier, the maternal Adèle Ratignolle, and Adèle's antithesis,
Mademoiselle Riesz. As these examples prove, literature is a place to
start in listening to the women who have given penetrating voice to an
often ignored experience in women's lives.

In the third chapter of this book, I investigate how working-class
writers use images of pregnancy as a way of carving out a place for
women's writing during the Depression. Margaret Sanger's *Motherhood
in Bondage* shows how early healthcare dealt with issues of pregnancy.
Sanger's collection of letters written by desperate women is a special
sort of literature, a collective cry against the abysmal state of women's
health in the early twentieth century. Meridel Le Sueur and Tillie Olsen
also included images of pregnancy in their works as a means of exploring how this lived experience merges with issues of class. These writers
were responding not only to the momentum that writers like Chopin had
created but also were writing against the male authors who positioned
working-class literature as a distinctly "male" environment, ignoring
the female perspective of the times. Paula Rabinowitz observes that

"women's labor created a different terrain—marked by sexual brutality, childbirth, and domestic work" (539). Sanger, Le Sueur, Olsen strove to highlight women's experience from their point of view in their narratives. Rabinowitz further argues that the "irruption of female sexuality and maternity into the discourse of proletarianism constructed female subjectivity within the interstices of class, gender, and sexuality" (542), thus serving to revise working class literature to include maternity and then pregnancy as important thematic concerns.

Certain African American female writers have chosen to write of pregnancy as the "fundamental challenge to identity" (206) that Julia Kristeva foregrounds as such in her essay "Women's Time." Is the experience, as Kristeva suggests, "a sort of instituted, socialized, natural psychosis" (206)? If so, then the idealized and/or absent images that have for so long prevailed implicitly or explicitly reject the tremendous opportunity offered by those that explore pregnancy as captivity. What motivates writers to acknowledge the torment and/or renewal that is often inspired by this transformation of the body and the mind? The texts selected for the fourth chapter illustrate the African American experience of pregnancy, most notably the mind/body connection and the friction that occurs as the pregnant body emerges. Harriet Jacobs' nineteenth-century text illustrates how African American pregnancy narratives often derive from their relationship to the slave narrative. Both Alice Walker's *The Color Purple* and *Meridian* touch on pregnancy and the relation that it has to a character's development, particularly in relation to racial issues. Toni Morrison's *The Bluest Eye*, like *The Color Purple*, treats the topic of pregnancy as the result of incest between fathers and daughters, before these works a topic rarely recorded in literature. With Morrison's *Beloved* we encounter a carefully illustrated labor and delivery scene that achieves a sort of "captivated" sensibility. At the turn of the century African American writer Sapphire continues thinking about the incest issue with regard to pregnancy and childbirth with her novel *Push*. What makes this more recent work stand out from those before it is the author's willingness to grapple with what become grim realities—social and economic—of pregnancy and childbirth, not solely the emotional realities.

Finally, I show the dramatic leaps that have been made since Kate Chopin took what I argue to be the first huge step towards opening up this discussion. I explore how this "memoir" differs from those of Naomi Wolf, Sandra Steingraber, Louise Erdrich and Carole Maso in an attempt to suggest that women have been able to challenge the imposed captivity of pregnancy so as to make it a time of reflection, productivity, and monumental questioning. The images in the works I study are inspired by an acute awareness of how the pregnant body is often held captive to the desires of others, notably authority figures such as husbands, the Church, or the medical establishment.

Critical to advancing this thesis is a look at *Blue Jay's Dance: A Birth Year*, Erdrich's empowering self-exploration of her own pregnancy. Erdrich's position as acclaimed writer and intellectual affords her a more relaxed relationship with her pregnant body, and she transforms the experience to an artistic one in an effort to dismiss any notions of captivity, as does Carole Maso in *The Room Lit by Roses: A Journal of Pregnancy and Birth*, a memoir that describes Maso's conception through the arrival of Rose, the daughter born to Maso and her partner, Helen. These memoirs of pregnancy are alike in their hopes of erasing cultural constraints put on pregnancy that have long inhibited a woman's self-determination regarding how such an experience might compromise or possibly enrich her both intellectually and philosophically.

Certainly these pregnancy narratives collide with advancements in medical technology and the ever-increasing desire to decipher pregnant bodies. The physical concerns of the body are typically exaggerated when the pregnant woman gives herself over to a healthcare provider who is more likely a classically trained physician than a mid-wife. Moreover, such technological breakthroughs as high-definition ultrasound and amniocentesis, ostensibly created to bring us closer to the growing fetus and to maximize care, have in some circumstances distanced the American woman from her own pregnancy. Karen L. Carr accuses the ultrasound, for example, in her "Optical Allusions: Hysterical Memories of and the Screening of Pregnant Sites," of being a tool that attempts "to investigate the deafness of the pregnant body by producing sight" (1), insistent on the woman's full disclosure of her "self." In such a protocol, the captive is allowed no mysterious knowledge that the captor is not privy to; in Rosalind Petchesky's words, ultrasound monitoring becomes "a kind of panoptics of the womb" (45). Carr also discusses how the ultrasound can be an effective tool in turning women away from abortion by personalizing the fetus and therefore holding the woman captive to an ideology that inhibits choice. Reclaiming autonomy of pregnancy, as these critics reveal, is terribly difficult with all of the technology that seeks to take it out of a woman's hands. Nevertheless, a reclamation of such autonomy through technology is possible. The hope is that these tools should, in fact, give a woman a clearer and more precise knowledge of her body so that she might take more of an active role in the pregnancy. If this is possible, then captivity (pregnancy) can be argued not only as less threatening than we imagine to subjectivity but also may be seen as a potentially valuable experience for the subject. While the history of women's reproductive health issues is of great importance to this book, there is not a review on this history or on the many changes that have been made with regard to these health issues. This study is concerned with how literature intersects with such a history, both informing and colliding with it. In looking at Sanger's *Motherhood in Bondage*, this work forecasts the collision of women's bodies with the medical establishment. Wharton's *Twilight Sleep* proves similarly evocative in the way that the author foregrounds the use of drug therapies in childbirth; and later, more contemporary memoirs like Wolf's, Steingraber's, Erdrich's and Maso's, whether intentionally or not, reveal a profound interaction between technological advancement and pregnant bodies.

The writers and texts selected represent a range of cultural, socio-economic, and intellectual backgrounds. The images of pregnancy are limited to American works because of their abundance and what would seem a similar desire among these particular writers to achieve emancipation of the body and the mind even across boundaries of race and class. Although popular contemporary works that deal with pregnancy are briefly touched on, the book is confined more to canonical literary works. *Captive Bodies* is organized in such a way as to highlight the different writers' responses to pregnancy. *How* class and race affect these writers' interpretation of the pregnant condition is discussed as well as the genres that these writers choose in which to interpret the condition. Throughout the book, how these different texts communicate similar notions of pregnancy as a captive state are considered.

Although the selected images studied do prompt plenty of questions about pregnant bodies as they are filtered through racial and social lenses, especially those in the chapter devoted to African American literature, the focus is to examine how these images read pregnant bodies as captive bodies. In addition, the treatment of how pregnant bodies differ according to race, class, and other social determiners is considered. *Captive Bodies* does not promise an extensive reading of all images of pregnancy in women's literature of the twentieth century. The authors represented here view pregnancy as a philosophically charged and potent experience. The intention is to delineate how such works explore pregnant bodies as captive and captivated bodies, and, in the (somewhat modified) words of Susan Bordo, to challenge "our conception and experience of our bodies, [by creating] a discourse that encourages us to 'imagine the possibilities' and close our eyes to limits and consequences" (39).

Notes

[1]Quoted in *Women's History* by Jone Johnson Lewis, About.com.

[2]To be sure the photo of Shields is heartening in the risk that she takes with her image in the way that she is photographed with very little cosmetic enhancement. Her normally chiseled features are softened and her arms defy the Hollywood "toned" effect. The *People* issue, on the other hand, gives credit to the celebrities who are able to deflate most swiftly, those whose bodies do not appear to have been "contaminated" by pregnancy and the distasteful fatness that accompanies it. *People* has quite a larger circulation base and so would, in turn, more likely penetrate the ideology of American culture.

[3]In her article entitled "Spying for Two," published Oct. 6, 2005 in *The New York Times*, Jodi Kantor remarks on the insertion of actress Jennifer Garner's real life pregnancy into the narrative of the show, how her pregnant body is not presented as a hindrance but rather as a powerful enhancement to Garner's character Sydney's arsenal of "disguises." Interestingly, though, ratings for the show dipped dramatically since Sydney's sexuality was dramatically pared down, and the character and the show was put to rest for good in May of 2006.

[4]Spears is featured on the cover dressed in a ball-gown, with hands primly posed on her lap. The pose and her facial expression is reminiscent of a Jacquie Kennedy still, while her hair calls to mind the platinum blond Marilyn Monroe. The inner spread is troubling in that she is photographed in a simulated, pink young girl's room. The contrast of her pregnant form with the room only emphasizes how ill-prepared she seems to be for this monumental transformation going on within her body and in her life.

CHAPTER 1

THE HISTORICAL FEMALE CAPTIVITY NARRATIVE AS PRECURSOR TO THE TWENTIETH-CENTURY PREGNANCY NARRATIVE

> I am valuable as a writer because I am a woman, because women,
> it seems to me, have some special knowledge about certain things.
> [It comes from] the ways in which they view the world, and from
> women's imagination. —Toni Morrison[1]

Just as the female captive might focus on physical scars acquired in captivity rather than confronting the emotional challenges, study of the pregnant body can easily be limited to noticing physical changes, and, in turn, we tend to overlook or deny the philosophical potential that such transformation might incite. In order to reach a point where we can come to understand pregnant bodies as philosophically charged objects of inquiry, we must acknowledge the restraints put on pregnant bodies and how such restriction might either enhance or compromise the knowledge that can erupt out of such an experience. A way to help establish a genre of pregnancy narratives, and, therefore, legitimizing such a study, is by analyzing how and why the historical female captivity narrative has emerged as one of the most intriguing genres garnering recent scholarly attention. To begin to refer to pregnant bodies as captive bodies or to classify pregnancy narratives as captivity narratives, it is helpful to study these captive narratives. Early American narratives depicting the captivity of Mary Rowlandson (1682), Hannah Dustan (1702), Mary Jemison (1824), and Sarah Wakefield (1864) have recently been appropriated by feminist scholars as a way into one important aspect of the female psyche of early America. These narratives have proven useful in helping us recognize how women's voices portray the subtle yet powerful way that the experience of mind and body under restraint shapes perception of both self and society.

Captivity narratives were read mainly, until the 1980s, as texts that illustrate a clash of cultures and the ultimate validation of the "superiority" of White laws and customs over Native American ones. Only recently have critics explored these texts for their subversive messages with close attention to how the women themselves reacted in captivity. Certainly elements of these four texts can be seen as figuring in important ways in various pregnancy narratives of the twentieth century; therefore, pregnancy narratives should be reexamined under a similar lens as the narratives of Rowlandson, Dustan, Jemison, and Wakefield, particularly in the ways that they share with these historical captivity narratives a similar experience of initial relinquishing of control followed by an ultimate redefinition of self in society. For the purposes of this study, which hereafter focuses more on twentieth-century pregnancy narratives, Rowlandson's narrative, as well as the other three lesser known narratives, provides a useful example of how one writes of an emotionally and physically restrictive episode in one's life while at the same time it teaches us to reevaluate the term "captivity."

According to critic Kathryn Zabelle Derounian-Stodola, the Indian captivity narrative "is arguably the first American literary form dominated by women's experiences as captives, storytellers, writers, and readers" (Intro xi). As sales and reviews of the book indicate, the American public became captivated by Rowlandson's tale, entitled *The Sovereignty and Goodness of God*. Its popular reception incited, in turn, a demand for a genre that included not only autobiographical accounts but fictitious ones as well that "involved the physical dangers of starvation and abuse; the spiritual dangers of pride and despair; and the psychological dangers of permanent emotional damage, depression, and guilt" (Rowlandson xxii). Although the captivity narrative initially circulated, as critic Christopher Castiglia notes, "to justify imperialistic expansion," he argues that it has also evolved into an important genre through which women can explore relationships "between race and gender, confinement and community, inscription and collective action" (2). Castiglia's *Bound and Determined* is one of several critical texts that have lately explored how female captivity narratives might be read profitably in the twenty-first century. He argues that the non-fictional captivity narrative "offers a story of female strength, endurance, and even prosperity" (4) by offering female authors a venue whereby they might channel their dissatisfaction with traditional women's roles. Most important to his study is Castiglia's assertion that captive women "have consistently used accounts of captivity to transgress and transform the boundaries of genre in order to accomplish their own ends" (4).

When taken into captivity, Rowlandson, Dustan, Jemison, and Wakefield are all without a doubt passive victims, similar to the pregnant woman as she loses control of a body over which she once enjoyed some power. Each narrative conveys varying degrees of authority that a captor might hold over the captive's body and mind. For instance, the documentation of Mary Rowlandson's 1676 captivity by Algonquin Indians becomes in her and her husband's hands a reclaiming of agency after a particularly bleak stripping of subjectivity. Rowlandson begins her narrative with a striking portrayal of the attack that lands her in captivity, carefully articulating "the dolefullest day that ever mine eyes saw" (cited in Derounian-Stodola 12). She writes not merely as one recounting an experience but as one still occupying a place in that experience, encouraging the reader through the use of present tense to take the journey alongside her: "Now away we must go with those Barbarous Creatures, with our bodies wounded and bleeding, and our hearts no less than our bodies" (cited in Derounian-Stodola 14). The seeming helplessness of Rowlandson's initial account betrays the impact that the experience has had on her life. As Michelle Burnham argues in *Captivity and Sentiment*, Mary Rowlandson's entrance into captivity, after witnessing relatives killed, herself injured and the child in her arms wounded by a bullet, "marks her transition into a physical and cultural homelessness that would resist psychological and ideological closure long after her experience of Indian captivity came to an end" (10). Burnham further explores how this experience profoundly affects Rowlandson's experience as a woman in early American society, noting that "Rowlandson's experience of liminality is not a process that takes place within a single culture but one that places her between two separate and distinct cultures...[,] between two systems of belief and ritual in a constant condition of the unexpected" (21).

Rowlandson's narrative became a bestseller, and there is little doubt that the rhetorical choices she makes within her narrative are in part responsible for this success. She recognizes both the universally held doubts and fears and the religious fervor of the times even as she manipulates her position as a female in a strikingly atypical situation. For instance, she speaks of the death of her young child with dire emotion: "my heart was overwhelmed with the thoughts of my condition," but she "[keeps] walking from one place to another" (18) in a stoic and practical attempt to survive. Thus, Rowlandson becomes constituted as potentially a heroic figure early on in the narrative, and, in turn, the reader empathizes with Rowlandson as she works out her emotions within the pages of her narrative. She then weaves a captivating tale of a woman using reserves of strength and fortitude previously unexplored in her natural patriarchal society. Ironically, what the many people reading her tale in early America did not perhaps realize was that Rowlandson's narrative was effectively rewriting, to some degree, a woman's position within that patriarchal hierarchy.

Rowlandson's account of her captivity is broken into twenty "removes," the word she chooses to describe each march to a new camp. These "removes" are useful in the narratives to underscore the hardships endured in each physical movement she makes with her captors. She writes of the physical as well as the emotional hardships, both of which require exceptional endurance. Rowlandson's narrative begins with her identifying herself with Job; she sees herself as the one who has been chosen both to experience and to tell the narrative of suffering and ultimate salvation. One might note how Rowlandson's voice becomes more authentically hers after the first few pages when she apparently begins to see this experience as singularly her own, unique in every way. In fact, Rowlandson begins to give voice to an impossible situation. The loss that she endures during this time—one child is maimed and shortly thereafter dies; the others are scattered and thus outside of her protective care—is horrifying. She meticulously records all of her frustrations, fears, and determinations for survival, knowing full well that this is quite possibly the defining experience in her life. It is to be endured in stages, in "removes," yet the further removed she is from her husband and her children, the more determined she is to survive within her new community. Interestingly, she makes reference to female relatives who ask to be put to death instead of being taken captive. Perhaps because of her Puritan faith in a God that has a plan or perhaps due to her unique strength of character (or perhaps both), Rowlandson instead reacts in an pragmatic way to her captivity, becoming, as Castiglia notes, part of the economy of her captive culture, employing her skills as a homemaker in order to exert some control, however limited, over her destiny.

Like an evangelist we might encounter on Sunday morning television, Rowlandson reveals a flair for the dramatic, and the reader is instantly engaged with her ability to recreate the tension surrounding her captivity. She first relies on the platitudes and usual descriptions of what her readers might expect from a captivity narrative—that is, she demonizes the Indians whom she labels "a company of hellhounds" and emphasizes the drama of her ordeal in crediting "the Lord [whose] Almighty power, preserved a number of us from death, for there were twenty-four of us taken alive: and carried Captive" (Derounian-Stodola 14). Rowlandson thus begins her narrative with only antipathy for her captors, and she employs menacing adjectives to describe them, calling them such names as "barbarous creatures, "ravenous Bears," and "Wolves." The constant derisive tone, however, soon shows ruptures. As early as the second remove Rowlandson relates how "one of the *Indians* [Rowlandson's italics, interestingly] carried my poor wounded Babe upon a horse" in order to give her a rest in the long journey (cited in Derounian-Stodola 15). Additionally, she relates another instance in which an Indian gives her a Bible and assures her that she will not be persecuted for studying it. It is in the sixth remove that Rowlandson begins to admit considerable admiration for the Indians' adaptive ways. Although she phrases this in a way that would seem to question why God would allow the "heathen" such order and prosperity, she nevertheless evidences a certain admiration for the way that, with careful attention in their daily travels, they evade the enemy. Not incidentally, the entire seventh remove is devoted to a minute description of the curious but inventive eating habits of her captors. She must admit that the Indians are skillful survivors in a harsh wilderness.

Rowlandson does wax philosophical at the end of her narrative, admitting to "have seen the extreme vanity of this World: one hour I have been in health, and wealth, wanting nothing: but the next hour in sickness, and wounds, and death, having nothing but sorrow and affliction" (cited in Derounian-Stodola 50). The reader might interpret this as mere appreciation at surviving her captivity and returning safely to her society. But it is more likely, given the wording in the aforementioned quote, that she has pondered how literal captivity is much the same as everyday life. Within her literal captivity, she experienced the same extreme highs and lows that she no doubt experienced as a woman in early America. She, in fact, quotes from the Bible what David says: "It is good for me that I have been afflicted" (cited in Derounian-Stodola 51). Though she couches her message in Biblical language appropriate for the times, her narrative reveals a revised understanding of the term "captivity." Captivity has challenged her to observe, name, analyze, and, finally, to write an authoritative account of life as she experienced it.

Although Rowlandson's husband purportedly had a heavy hand in shaping the rhetorical framing of her narrative, evident in the document is such extreme attention to detailing even the most mundane experiences of her captivity that she was undeniably insisting on being the author of at least part of her story. On an immediate level of intention, Rowlandson apparently needed to complete a detailed document in order to dispel any notion that she might have been raped in captivity. If suspicions of rape had persisted, her return to society would have been more complicated. Today we are newly confronted with women in combat, and so we find ourselves in much the same predicament with regard to female captives' return to society.[2] Captivity narratives (especially female ones) are ripe for public consumption for a variety of reasons, one being that they can become unifying national narratives—venues through which we might vicariously play with ideas of restriction and resistance, but they can also play a subversive role, reawakening us to truths about ourselves that we might not want to confront. Rowlandson's narrative has for centuries served as a unifying narrative, but Rowlandson's narrative is useful, alternately, in feminist discourse. Clearly she believes her captivity to be a brief "remove" from her role as subservient wife and doting mother, and the language she uses shows her to be voicing both significant loss and monumental gain. In her retelling of her captivity, Rowlandson also provides future writers of pregnancy narratives with a useful format through which to recount an experience of captivity, and the sheer popularity of her narrative and the fame that it has garnered her problematizes how historians continue to want to frame her—as a simple, devout, and subservient wife and mother.

Just as pregnancy narratives come in variations on two themes—either championing the experience or denigrating it—there are also huge discrepancies between the various historical captivity narratives. Hannah Dustan's narrative, first published in 1697, is perhaps the most curious tale of a woman taken captive. When Abenaki Indians attacked and entered Hannah Dustan's home in 1697, she was confined to her bed after just having given birth, made to watch the murder of her newborn, and then dragged numerous miles by her captors. This loss of agency was merely temporary, however. Cotton Mather gives voice to Dustan's captivity, describing how she persuaded her midwife and a young boy to assist her in killing and scalping their captors (Derounian-Stodola 55). Mather recognized Dustan's experience as one with powerful religious rhetorical appeal and also one useful to his community as a unifying national narrative. No doubt Dustan's experience was terrifying to many early Americans—more specifically, male Americans—since although she did successfully defend her own life against the "savages" who took her captive, she is depicted at the same time as a woman who is capable of transgressive acts, effectively removing her from the "demure" and submissive female role of the times. Mather chooses to whitewash the obvious disturbing nature of her actions and instead writes of Dustan's actions as heroic, carefully constructing the episode (indeed, relying on the very Old Testament prescription of "an eye for an eye") as an act of "communal providence" (55).

It is fascinating how Dustan is positioned by Mather as one who acts with nationalistic purpose and passion, saving not only her own life but proving the inherently savage nature of the Native Americans. So intense is Mather's determination to use Dustan's act as a legitimization of acts of aggression against Native Americans that he is careful to paint Dustan as a sympathetic, maternal being, noting that Dustan is taken "having lain-in about a Week" (58)—meaning that she has just given birth a week earlier. Mather then creates a suspenseful and concise narrative of a woman who witnesses "furious Tawnies coming into the House," watching as the "raging Dragons rifle[d] all they could carry away" (58). In order to prepare the reader for the brutality of Dustan's actions later in the narrative, Mather carefully relates the violent actions that prefigure her own, noting that Dustan watches as the "Savages would presently Bury their Hatchets in [the White settlers'] Brains, and leave their Carcasses on the Ground for Birds and Beasts to Feed upon" (59). Further, Dustan is characterized as superhuman in her ability to withstand the hardships of a postpartum condition while traveling numerous miles with her captors. Not surprisingly, Mather recounts her actions in a way that legitimizes them by likening them to the biblical acts of Jael upon Sisera. Further underscoring how politically motivated Mather's agenda truly was, Michelle Burnham notes how narratives like Dustan's "fulfilled a nationalist function particularly effectively, largely because so many of the women taken captive were mothers whose bodies quite literally reproduced the nation and therefore had to be preserved" (52). Moreover, Burnham argues that Dustan's narrative encouraged readers "to identify with the captive mother [in an attempt to] veil her violent act of agency beneath the urgency of this reproductive necessity" (52).

Dustan's narrative proves an interesting one to study as a precursor to pregnancy narratives that are meant to guide the reader towards a certain set of emotions; such texts are typically either written by men who desire to interpret the experience in a certain way or by an established group of people who seek to shape a woman's understanding of the pregnant body. While Rowlandson did at least participate in the writing of her narrative, Dustan's comes to us courtesy of Cotton Mather who, by all accounts, used her story for a specific purpose. She becomes doubly captive, then—both literally the captive and figuratively the captive to Mather's and, by extension, America's understanding of her captivity. An alternative reading of Dustan's narrative demands that we notice the absence of Dustan's voice within the narrative and how this is perhaps the most rhetorically profound aspect of it. Such an absence of her authentic or uncensored voice suggests that there is another embedded narrative beneath Mather's, and we can only conjecture as to what that narrative might be. Without a doubt, Dustan's experience in captivity is loaded with explosive possibility. Hers is a story about a woman who organizes and successfully enacts a murderous rampage, effectively turning the tables on her captors. Strangely, what Mather focuses on is how he might shape the tale into one of "anti-Indian propaganda" and "Christian piety" (Burnham 52). That he does not write her behavior as threatening reflects his confidence in the fact that her story is completely under his thumb; such dismissal of female agency is later reflected in pregnancy literature in the way that male writers write pregnancy either by avoiding the subject altogether or by minimizing the monumental transformations that might erupt from it. Although Dustan's voice is noticeably absent from Mather's text, according to an interview with Dustan in her later life, she ultimately viewed her captivity as "the central event of her life" (cited in Derounian-Stodola 56) and later purportedly wrote privately of her captivity as spiritually cleansing.

Though it is debatable to what degree Dustan's experience in captivity changed her life, there is absolutely no doubt with regard to how captivity reshaped the direction of Mary Jemison's life. Jemison was born on her parents' voyage from Ireland to a settlement in Pennsylvania, and in 1758, when Jemison was fifteen, she was taken by a Shawnee and French raiding party and given to two Seneca women to replace a lost family member. Jemison's 1824 narrative (a bestseller like Rowlandson's) was and remains intriguing to readers precisely because, unlike Rowlandson and Dustan, she declined numerous offers to return to white society.[3] In fact, Jemison married into the Seneca tribe, an act that solidified her identity as a Seneca woman, also an act that "made a return to white society less desirable and she backs her decision to stay by referring to her family network of three living children, thirty-nine grandchildren, and fourteen great-grandchildren" (Derounian-Stodola 120). Jemison's narrative of her captivity and transculturation quite obviously became "a matter of interest and curiosity" (Derounian-Stodola 125) to early Americans. Labeled "The White Woman," Jemison recognized the power that she held in allowing her story to be written for public consumption.[4] Derounian-Stodola's introductory commentary on Jemison's narrative credits Jemison as a woman adept at "textual manipulation" (Derounian-Stodola 120), expertly using her story in a way that both "ennoble[s] the Senecas [and] discredit[s] the whites" (Derounian-Stodola 121).

The preface to Jemison's narrative, written by James Everett Seaver, purports to recognize the importance of the ensuing story, promising the reader that the narrative will show "what trials may be surmounted; what cruelties perpetrated, and what pain endured, when stern necessity holds the reins" (Derounian-Stodola 119).[5] Further, Derounian-Stodola notes that at the end of Jemison's narrative, she "reiterates her position as matriarch within Seneca culture and revalidates and drives the car of fate" (Derounian-Stodola 123). To his credit, Seaver recognizes the potential importance of the document (carefully noting his own avoidance of prolixity and exaggeration), but he fails to acknowledge how Jemison's powerful voice, coupled with her transgressive act, marks a significant rupture in the discourse of female captivity. Jemison has committed the unthinkable act in a culture that is taught to be suspicious of the "other"; moreover, in marrying into the Seneca tribe, she has made a return to white society virtually impossible. In Seaver's interpretation, he attempts to impose certain values on her narrative, values that do not seem to reflect her account of captivity and transculturation at all.[6] Nevertheless, Jemison's literal act of turning captivity into a positive revisioning of female experience has unlimited potential for other women writers who might refigure other "captive" experiences (like pregnancy) as initiating astonishing acts of agency.

Jemison's narrative differs perhaps most substantially from other female captivity narratives in its refusal to rely on the religious rhetoric so often characteristic of these texts. Jemison was taken at an early age but not so young that she does not recall the religious emphasis that shaped the early years with her birth parents. In fact, she writes that in the early days of her captivity, she was prone to recite prayers her mother had taught her, but she also notes that such prayers "have long since [been] forgotten" (134). Her growing ambivalence towards the Bible and other religious doctrine is, thus, pronounced and underlines the dramatic distance between her life before captivity and her life afterwards. Though she mentions with a pleasant reference a missionary who once gave her a Bible, she admits to reading it rarely.

Jemison enters captivity in much the same fashion as do Rowlandson and Dustan (except, of course, she is at a much younger age), is made to watch atrocities committed against relatives and neighbors, and within her narrative she admits to feeling "a kind of horror, anxiety, and dread" (137). But, her narrative soon turns into one in which she, too, recognizes her captors as family. They adopt her into their tribe to replace a lost tribe member, and she starts to feel included as such. Her growing ambivalence toward Christianity, in turn, underscores her total immersion into life with her tribe. As stated earlier, Jemison uses her narrative as a way to increase awareness about her tribe, to commend certain behaviors, and to offer an alternative representation of a people who were for so long despised and persecuted by whites.[7] Like Rowlandson, Jemison makes a point of recording feelings of powerlessness as to her fate early in the captivity experience, but Jemison's feelings of uncertainty subside when she is ceremonially "adopted" by the Indians. Obviously, this ceremony has a profound effect on Jemison, and she chooses this anecdote as a starting point for detailing certain customs of her tribe, essentially serving to humanize the Indians and thus to dignify her choice to remain with them. In fact, the majority of the narrative is about her life with the Senecas, and, actually, the reader is somewhat jolted by the abrupt presentation of her taking up life as a Seneca woman: she marries, has a child, loses her first husband, and marries again all within a few pages. Jemison's narrative is important to this study in the way that it defies certain notions of what constitutes the "traditional historical female captivity narrative." Jemison's tale explodes the term "captivity" in that she literally becomes "captivated by" her captors, thus becoming the living embodiment of how captivity might positively shape a life. Indeed, the narrative of her captivity becomes one about growing independence and self-direction. Jemison, much more so than Rowlandson before her, realizes that her captivity is uncharacteristically freeing in certain ways. Not only is the Indian culture more willing to allow a woman to rise in the ranks, but also she is able to realize authority in life choices, illustrated, for example, as Christopher Castiglia writes, in "the large degree of economic self-governance she achieves among the Indians" (36). Castiglia further notes that "rather than supplying the narrative of victimization and brutalization ... Jemison uses her story to reimagine women's 'proper' spaces" (35).

Sarah Wakefield's narrative of her captivity in 1862 is less well known than the aforementioned narratives, but it is nonetheless important as a tale of female agency and another telling example of transformation through experience. The actual writing of the narrative is fueled by Wakefield's indignation at the way that a patriarchal society attempts to exploit her experience, choosing to view her as a victim rather than as a survivor.[8] Using simple words, Wakefield writes in her preface that her reader should not expect her story to "please the mind's fancy" (241). Instead, her impetus to write is clearly didactic in nature, meant, in her words, "to vindicate myself, as I have been grievously abused by many, who are ignorant of the particulars of my captivity and release by the Indians" (241). Derounian-Stodola's introductory commentary emphasizes Wakefield's understanding of Christianity as doing unto others as she would be done and of her captivity which she views as a direct result of the American government's acting unfairly against the Dakotas, thus inciting the Dakota War in 1862.[9] Her inability to save Chaska, her Dakota protector, motivates her desire to narrate "the story of his sacrifice for posterity" (239). Further, Wakefield apparently insisted on writing and publishing her own narrative in order to circumvent those who might manipulate her text and thus alter her rendition of her own captivity. Derounian-Stodola likens Wakefield to an early Oskar Schindler or a Hugh C. Thompson, men who spoke out in defense of innocents whose lives were threatened. It is obvious, though, that Wakefield's attempts to revise certain notions about the Indians were more daunting than theirs given her rather low position in society. Most notably, Wakefield's narrative resembles the contemporary pregnancy narrative in its fierce refusal to give into traditional definitions of captivity. Wakefield's experience in captivity brings about surely the most definitive actions that she has ever taken. The fearlessness and confidence in which she takes on the establishment in an attempt to save the lives of Native Americans underscore the monumental effect that this experience has had on her life.

Pregnancy narratives accomplish, in the twentieth and twenty-first centuries, something similar to that of the captivity narrative by likewise "writing a new subjectivity, using different grammars of identification" (Castiglia 7). Pregnancy narratives, like their earlier counterparts in the captivity tradition, destabilize certain fixed notions about maternity, the pregnant body, and a woman's capability of giving voice to her individual experiences. Perhaps the most profound similarity between historical female captivity narratives and pregnancy narratives is their mutual fascination with the female psyche as it endures uncommon restraint, and the authors of both types of narratives are invested in studying the surprising insight that results from this restraint. Castiglia writes that "captive white women have shown that while they are never free, they have nevertheless developed voices with which to denaturalize and revise their home cultures' scripts of identity and to rearticulate American genres, popular rhetoric, and mythology so as to speak the experiences of those marginalized by the dominant national language" (12). The pregnancy narrative (both fictional and non-fictional) of the twentieth century similarly shows a tension between the accepted progression the pregnant body takes as dictated by the healthcare provider and the more intuitive notion of growth and enlightenment that the experiencing subject is likely to feel. Might we, then, extend the same hope of self-realization for women living in the physically and emotionally captive condition of pregnancy that some early American readers did for female captives?

Fascination with captivity narratives over the centuries is much like our fascination with the pregnant condition. Those who do not endure captivity have little or no understanding of what goes on inside the head of the captive. Just what exactly was Mary Rowlandson thinking as she endured day after day of physical and emotional restriction in an environment considerably different from her native one? Consider also what it is like to inhabit a body that is in the process of doubling itself. As noted by feminist philosophers Iris Marion Young and Julia Kristeva, pregnancy, at the very least, transforms a woman's interaction with her physical body, and it might potentially explode her philosophical understanding of such by complicating the mind/body connection. One reason for historical female captivity narratives' great popularity at the time of their initial publication is the fact that they implicitly or explicitly foregrounded the female body. The fact that there is always the potential for violation within captivity naturally affects and sensationalizes the narrative. Mary Rowlandson is careful to dispel any notion that she is violated while in captivity; in fact, she must draw attention away from her body in order to tell her story. Writers of pregnancy narratives must similarly acknowledge that sight of the pregnant body captivates the public. That the public might be "captivated by" the pregnant body, however, implies perhaps too positive an attention. In fact, the general public is more typically not drawn to but rather embarrassed or repulsed by such swelling. Therefore, writers of pregnancy narratives have the enormous task of transforming public response to (and a woman's own feelings about) the pregnant body.

Captivity certainly has more negative connotations than does pregnancy, but both are states of being wherein self-authority is ostensibly denied, wherein time often blurs, and independent choice is compromised. Just as there are various stages or removes that a captive must endure, a pregnancy is likewise broken down into stages, often depicted as one increasingly difficult struggle after another. June Namias classifies the female captive into several categories based upon how the women reacted in captivity. She refers to Rowlandson as a "Survivor," a woman who "experiences and feels a wide range of stress, but ultimately adapts to, tries to make sense of, and comes to terms with her situation" (29). Namias stresses that Rowlandson's narrative "proved that a woman could find ways to gain control over her life ... [and] could muster religious, physical, social, and psychological resources on her own" (47-8). Michelle Burnham notes, in turn, that female captives often "indulge[d] in transgressive behavior or enact[ed] forms of resistant agency, not in spite of their captivity but precisely as a result of it" (3). She believes that the sentimentality with which many read these narratives necessarily compromises the impact that these accounts could have had on the furthering of female agency: "sentimental discourse at once conceals the movement across such boundaries and legitimizes the transgressive female agency produced by it" (4). Christopher Castiglia observes that tales of captivity allowed women writers to articulate for themselves and their readers situations in which they were in control, to generate a sort of feminist discourse that would have otherwise been widely discouraged. Indeed, it seems that the sentimental façade of these narratives proved useful in attracting a wider audience for these writers; today, however, we can see past the sentimentality of a tale like Rowlandson's to the more palimpsestic text of her own interpretation of experience. Castiglia further explores the way that historical female captives experienced a liminal state of being. He notices how these narratives are framed as "liminars," telling the story of the women's balance between identifying with their home culture and experiencing some sort of bond with their captors. This liminality has a great deal of resonance in pregnancy narratives as the woman's interaction with the growing fetus resembles a captive/captor relationship and is often what instigates serious philosophical thought about authority over one's own body.

Just as Rowlandson writes herself as a savior of her community through the payment for all of their sins in her endured captivity, Iris Marion Young argues that there is potential for claiming a similar sense of value in reading pregnancy as captivity. She observes that even though our society often "devalues and trivializes women, regards women as weak and dainty, the pregnant woman can gain a certain sense of self respect" (166) in recognizing that she has been able to find a place wherein she is liberated from "the sexually objectifying gaze that alienates and instrumentalizes her in her nonpregnant state" (167). Like the pregnant woman who is temporarily displaced from what can only be considered a patriarchal space by becoming desexualized, the literal captive is, in Rowlandson's, Dustan's, Jemison's, or Wakefield's case, taken away from a society that allows her only a subservient role. Both "captives" must learn to live successfully in these alternate spheres. Each captivity narrative detailed in this chapter illustrates the individuality with which each of the women reacted to her conditions. Although the reactions differ in many ways, they are similar in their deviation from prescribed roles a woman might enact in early America. These narratives could, then, be viewed profitably as precursors to the contemporary pregnancy narrative in the confidence they exude in detailing a profoundly emotionally and physically restrictive condition. Young describes pregnancy in the following manner: "The pregnant woman experiences herself as a source and participant in a creative process. Though she does not plan and direct it, neither does it merely wash over her; rather, she is this process, this change. Time stretches out, moments and days take on a depth because she experiences more changes in herself, her body.

Each day, each week, she looks at herself for signs of transformation" (167). Various critics have concluded that literal captivity sparked the same sense of enervation and resplendent possibility in these four early American women. Their tales, arguably, made pregnancy narratives possible and certainly encourage a reading of pregnancy narratives as modern-day captivity tales. The voices within these various narratives demonstrate an awareness of the interests of their reading audience and an understanding that the result of transcription is necessarily a journey towards self-definition. Another shared characteristic of the narratives is a crucial desire to transmit unique experience to others and to have these words define the experience as one that is both about themselves and the world at large.

Pregnancy narratives are by their very existence transgressive. They recount a time period that is often referred to as "confinement," dismissed for many years as a topic unfit for discussion. Both the traditional clothing for and mindset surrounding pregnancy are meant to cover up or minimize both the grand scale and the largeness of pregnant bodies and the worldly introspection that might be a natural result of the experience. Though the details that underscore the traditional captivity tale are characteristic also of the pregnancy narrative, the true similarity between the two lies in the impetus to write and re-explore each of these experiences of captivity. To be sure, literal captivity is a state of being that most know little about. Pregnancy is another of those elusive states of being. Unless one experiences pregnancy, one has little idea of the dramatic physiological and psychological transformations that take place during this nine-month period. Curiosity about historical captivity narratives has been and continues to be high, but, strangely, curiosity about pregnancy (beyond the obvious physical, that is) and the attempts to "write" the experience have remained oddly low. We are just beginning to realize the importance of these early American narratives to feminist studies. Pregnancy narratives are similarly precious storehouses of potential that need not gather dust for the next three hundred years.

The following chapter analyzes twentieth-century texts by several of the century's most esteemed women writers whose works suggest that pregnancy narratives are much more than documentary accounts of clinical gestation. *Captive Bodies* now moves from an analysis of historical accounts of the literal captivity of several women of the seventeenth, eighteenth, and nineteenth centuries to the twentieth century, and, arguably, to studying on a more figurative level how pregnancy narratives reveal themselves to be subtle yet cunning documents reflecting the poignant and powerful reactions women have to conditions of captivity.

Notes

[1]From "An Interview with Toni Morrison, Hessian Radio Network, Frankfurt, Germany," conducted by Rosemarie K. Lester. Reprinted in *Critical Essays on Toni Morrison* (Boston: G. K. Hall and Co., 1988), pp. 47-54.

[2]The April 1, 2003, cover of *Newsweek* magazine contains the photo of Private Jessica Lynch, the American soldier rescued from captivity in an Iraqi hospital. That this story served as a unifying national narrative during "Operation Iraqi Freedom" is beyond question.

[3]Jemison's experience of captivity was told to James Everett Seaver, who, in turn, recorded and saw to the publication of her experience. Jemison recognized the potential for manipulation of the much sought-after tale of her life and therefore demanded that her trusted friend Thomas Clute be in attendance at the transcriptions of her story. That Jemison's tale is told in first-person suggests that she is in some control of the narrative.

[4]The introduction to her narrative functions to give the reader a clear picture of Jemison's physical appearance and character, to satisfy the curiosity of those who would be reading her narrative, and to show that she does indeed conform to the Native American ways even though her countenance is that of an Irish-American.

[5]Derounian-Stodola notes in her introductory commentary that Jemison's experience is by no means the only narrative of transculturation, but the other narratives "do not seem to have penetrated their editorialized narratives as strongly as Jemison's, which makes her text particularly significant" (121).

[6]Christopher Castiglia notices that Seaver prepares the reader for the many injustices that Jemison experienced among the Indians, but Castiglia argues that a careful reading of the actual narrative shows her treatment by the Indians to be fair and her acceptance total and complete. The only ill treatment comes at the hands of whites, most notably a white man who attempts to pass himself off as a relative in an attempt to gain some of her land.

[7]Early in the narrative Jemison notes the skill with which the Senecas travel without detection, by replacing each weed they tread, never holding a bush or limb and never breaking one in order to "completely elude their pursuers" (137). This is one of many anecdotes meant to allude to the craftiness of her tribe.

[8]Wakefield had a protector in captivity, a Dakota named Chaska who saved Wakefield and her children numerous times from harm.

[9]Derounian-Stodola's preface to Wakefield's narrative beginning on page

237 in *Women's Indian Captivity Narratives* describes how during the six-week war, the Dakotas killed close to five hundred white soldiers and settlers and took more than two hundred white and mixed-blood captives. Wakefield writes that the entire conflict might have been avoided had the U.S. government given the Indians the food rations that they owed them.

CHAPTER 2

LEGITIMIZING CAPTIVITY:
PREGNANCY FROM CHOPIN TO O'CONNOR

Are we bad women, bad mothers, for exploring such issues?
Should pregnancy and birth remain such sanitized rites of passage that we can't speak graphically or honestly about them? I
believe not.

—Naomi Wolf[1]

There is no proof that Kate Chopin's inclusion of the pregnancy narrative
in her most controversial text *The Awakening* prompted later women
writers to consider the pregnant condition as worthy philosophical
fodder, but after so many centuries of the omission of such narratives,
Chopin must be acknowledged for at least causing a critical rupture in
the discourse surrounding pregnancy and for prompting future writers to enter into the conversation. Her comrades in a similar endeavor,
among them Charlotte Perkins Gilman, Edith Wharton, and Flannery
O'Connor, seem to have picked up where Chopin left off. Though
not usually recognized for their contributions in developing discourse
about pregnancy, the writers included in this chapter are now critically
regarded as authorities on many aspects of twentieth-century experience
and, arguably, the distinctive nature of female experience in a society
often hostile towards progressive strides for women. This chapter clari-
fies the importance of these authors' forwarding of a pregnancy genre
and their encouraging and generating a varied and transgressive body
of work that has further opened the doors for more women writers to
explore the captive pregnant body and its relationship to American society. What is most valuable about these writers is how they offer such a
range of perspectives on pregnancy, moving from ambivalence to irony
to celebration to condemnation. Beginning with the established classic
The Awakening and then moving to understudied works like Gilman's
Herland, Wharton's *Twilight Sleep*, and O'Connor's "A Stroke of Good

Fortune" reveals a quiet but powerful series of moments in the emergence of a new genre in American literature.

Chopin's *The Awakening* is no longer under-evaluated in terms of its literary merit or even its potential impact in feminist discourse, though perhaps the pregnancy narrative within the text has not been mined sufficiently for the ways that it follows in the captivity tradition. When we note how traditional images of pregnancy were then typically written, with woman as beaming Madonna, full and ripe with child, we might begin to appreciate how difficult it must have been for American women writers to revise such an idealized image of pregnancy. Despite obstacles, Chopin, with *The Awakening*, begins a timely revision of these earlier images of pregnancy, images that either glorified or ignored the condition entirely. Critic Patricia Hopkins Lattin refutes the argument that Chopin produced only idealized images of motherhood, noting that "although in some stories Chopin's views of childbirth and motherhood appear conventional, suggesting that becoming a mother has a strong positive potential, this is true almost entirely in stories in which a woman either will never have a child or has not had one" (8).[2] Chopin may be considered, then, the pivotal writer of this study for many reasons, the most important being that she opens the door for women writers of the twentieth century to begin to discuss candidly both the joys of and apprehensions about pregnancy and childbirth.

Entering the world of the "mother-woman" of *The Awakening*, Adèle Ratignolle and not, strangely, the text's main character Edna Pontellier, we encounter a third-person narration that objectively follows Adèle's pregnancy and childbirth. Here, as in other texts I will study, we note the importance of looking at secondary characters and how they enrich the narrative. On the surface, Chopin's presentation of pregnancy appears to resemble earlier male representations, emphasizing the positive only in order to reaffirm the subjugated position of the female body in American society. Closer study suggests, however, that Chopin's portrayal of Adèle offers the reader a chance to look at her pregnant body as a captive body reacting, oftentimes aggressively, to impositions that society has placed on it. It is no mystery that Edna Pontellier remains one of the more elusive and enigmatic characters in twentieth-century literature. Curiously, however, critics take a simplistic attitude toward Chopin's intentions with regard to Adèle's character.[3] Early in the narrative the narrator discusses the qualities of the "mother-women" of Grand Isle and singles out Adèle as the "embodiment of every womanly grace and charm" (10), painting a picture of a woman fully and happily immersed in the role of wife and mother, rather blind to her own wants and desires.

Despite her obvious charm and dedication in the maternal arena, in the end when we are allowed into Adèle's birthing room, we are forced to see a more complicated side of her said "grace" and "charm" and, thus, to reconsider certain critics' attempts to trivialize or dismiss Adèle. It is difficult to fathom given Chopin's careful construction of Edna Pontellier that she would create such a predictably drawn character as Adèle Ratignolle is often read to be. In fact, Edna would not have been as interesting had she not been written against equally complex characters like both Adèle and Mademoiselle Riesz.

Chopin offers, in these three female characters, a composite of the possibilities inherent in the female gender, but these possibilities also intersect, making each character all the more fascinating. Mademoiselle Riesz, for example, is the aesthete, "a disagreeable little woman, no longer young" (Chopin 32), who seemingly sacrifices all personal involvement for her music, never considering pregnancy or motherhood as an artistic or otherwise fulfilling enterprise. Such a summation, however, is undoubtedly too pat given the limited access we have to her character and the motivations behind her choices. Indeed, Chopin does write that she was seen "at intervals objecting to the crying of a baby, which a nurse in the adjoining cottage was endeavoring to put to sleep" (32), but Mademoiselle Riesz's deep interest in Edna's incipient awakening to artistic enterprise and sexual satisfaction shows her to have a stake in more than her music. Ostensibly, Adèle is Mademoiselle Riesz's diametric opposite as she seems to represent the ideal Creole mother with and from whom Edna is clearly both fascinated and repulsed, but a closer analysis reveals Madame Ratignolle and Mademoiselle Riesz to be in pursuit of a similar recognition. Mademoiselle Riesz, in fact, defines an artist at one point in the text as one who possesses "the courageous soul...that dares and defies" (84). Arguably, she and Adèle have come to understand themselves more fully than Edna has and enjoy a certain amount of peace in their respective roles, but both women are also performers who are attempting to rewrite—subtly and not so subtly—the rules of the "cult of true womanhood." While readers may see distinct ways that both Mademoiselle Riesz and, later, Edna strives to embody the definition that Mademoiselle Riesz stipulates for the artist, Adèle's pursuit of artistic endeavor is largely ignored by most critics. Given that Adèle superficially fits the model her society has laid out for her, always angelically figured, clad in stark white and ruffles to highlight her "more feminine and matronly figure" (145), she is often dismissed as either a potent endorsement for mindless maternity or, as Edna finally seems to see her, as an effective warning as to the captivity that awaits a woman of child-bearing age. Without rejecting fully either interpretation, Chopin's portrayal of Adèle is far more complicated than it seems at first glance, that, actually, Chopin depicts Adèle as trying to perform her pregnancy in an attempt to legitimize it as an artistic enterprise in itself.

Adèle is, from the first, not a silly, vapid character; on the contrary, she has some of the most revelatory and contemplative lines in the text. Edna is quite taken with her, spends ample time studying her, and realizes her importance in the community; moreover, Edna is both intrigued by Adèle's Creole candor yet mystified by her perfect chastity and femininity. Adèle is a woman who seemingly revels in her "condition," relishing the attention that it naturally grants her, appearing at times to be willingly captivated by her captivity. While it may seem that she has submitted totally to her temporarily captive state, her devotion to her "roles" as pregnant Madonna and devoted mother is less a marker of blind acceptance of pregnancy as inevitability than an explicit choice on her part to explore both the joys inherent in that role and the potentially restrictive nature of it. From the outset of the novel she is pregnant, though not obviously so; as the narrator relates to the reader, "no one would have known a thing about it but for her persistence in making it the subject of conversation" (11). That is, she continually interjects her pregnancy into conversation, even entertaining "old Monsieur Farival [with] the harrowing story of one of her accouchements" and, much to Edna's horror, "withhold[s] no intimate detail" (12). She insists, then, on acknowledgment of her unique condition; she "writes" it into everyday discourse. Further, Adèle resists the confinement often expected of a pregnant woman of her era by remaining "rather desirous of joining in the general and animated conversation which was still in progress" (58) in the late summer nights on Grand Isle. In fact, were she to follow "advice" on acceptable behavior for pregnant women of her time, like that, for example, of Dr. George Naphey in 1869, she would adopt the attitude that "walking is the best exercise" but would strongly oppose dancing due to fear of hurting the fetus.[4] As far as Dr. Naphey's guide is concerned, while Adele walks at night under protective cover of dusk, she also rebels in numerous ways and is bold enough, in a time famous for evasion of the truth, to confront Robert Lebrun about his intentions toward Edna. In fact, her pregnant body in a certain way legitimizes the bluntness of her words to Robert. As Iris Marion Young observes about others' projections toward her own pregnant body, the rather desexualized nature of Adèle's body in pregnancy allows her to voice certain opinions about sexual engagement that at any other time she might refrain from expressing. In her attempts to remain a part of the community, to resist being relegated to the fringe because of her condition, we can see her trying to insert her pregnancy and her understanding of sexual desire into the discourse as a valid and valuable subject. There are certainly a number of times when she is told to "rest," but she always seems busy, either in her sewing or in conversation. Furthermore, there is evidence that Adèle prepares herself for the psychological turmoil involved in the last stages of pregnancy. When she fails to join her husband at Edna's dinner party and he leaves early, Chopin relates that his reason for leaving was that "[Adèle] was filled with vague dread, which only her husband's presence could allay" (118), suggesting that she, in fact, is attempting to maintain the requisite strength for childbirth. Evidence like this in Chopin's text supports the idea that not only does Adèle view her pregnancies as performances that grant her attention, but she also recognizes pregnancy to be monumental in the sense that a woman's mind and body must confront simultaneously granting another life while losing subjectivity.

Since the central focus of *The Awakening* is directed at Edna's sexual and emotional awakening during which she must withdraw dramatically from her maternal role, Adèle's continued attempts to call attention to her condition seem on occasion pathetic if one equates feminism with a rejection of all things maternal. Though it is frustrating to some to read how Adèle's other talents, like piano-playing, become to her only marginal interests that "she was keeping up ... on account of the children, she said, because she and her husband both considered it a means of brightening the home and making it more attractive" (31), I would argue that Chopin is careful to avoid a reductionist reading of Adèle. Peggy Skaggs' 1985 study entitled *Kate Chopin* devotes a large section to *The Awakening* and even further segues into a study of Adèle Ratignolle. Her summation of Adèle is problematic but predictable given the political atmosphere in which Skaggs' book was written. Skaggs reiterates the position that to live life as a "mother-woman" is a life only half-lived. Even as she relates that "Chopin sees an absolutely inescapable link—basic, natural, and powerful—between the female identity and motherhood" (90), Skaggs does not want to venture down that rather complicated path; instead, she wants to point out the many ways that Adèle represents "the short-comings of a person settling for less than full development as a human being" (91). In order to further this argument, Skaggs points out what she refers to as Adèle's "flaws"—first and foremost, her "preoccupation with her 'condition'" (92). Characteristic of certain feminisms of the seventies and eighties is an exaggerated effort to sweep the experiences of pregnancy and childbirth under the rug, to act as if they are not legitimate "preoccupations" and concerns.[5] Particularly distasteful to Skaggs (and to numerous other critics) is the way that Adèle approaches the experience of childbirth "as her moment of glory to be savored to the fullest" (93). Could we not, however, read Adèle's discussions of and anxious anticipation of the childbirth to be an attempt to write herself out of a captive condition, when tradition encourages that she act demurely and remain patiently resigned to what so many read as a commonplace and therefore philosophically mundane experience? A contemporary reader, one interested in reading pregnancy and childbirth as valid and potentially self-fulfilling experiences in and of themselves, might read Adèle's subtle insertions of her body into everyday discourse as a way of giving presence to her experience. For example, she attempts to validate her condition by defying the norms of the culture when she goes to see Edna when she is supposed to be hiding out in confinement. Skaggs' derisive tone in speaking of how Adèle later wrings "every possible ounce of attention" from her "hour of trial" (94) suggests that Adèle's attentiveness to her pregnancy, a state she ostensibly sees as a sensory heightening on both an emotional and physical level, is not in fact worthwhile. Skaggs ends her analysis with the announcement that "a healthy sense of [Adèle's] own worth would surely lead her to object to this biennial suffering," (94), but in such a declaration Skaggs assumes that nothing can be gained from such experiences, even if they require exceptional fortitude and endurance. Surely this is not the case, as later pregnancy narratives suggest.

In fact, Chopin does create a case for viewing Adèle's successive pregnancies and childbirths—her "trials," if you will—as performances akin to Mademoiselle Riesz's concerts; perhaps they grant her a position of prominence where she might only experience marginality. In fact, her pregnancies become central to her character, and these "performances" non-verbally dismiss what many women would see as a correlation between confinement and maternity. For instance, she invites Edna to witness the birth in order to legitimize it as a valid experience, to record it, in sharp contrast to Edna's own births which were erased due to the infringement of the medical establishment. Edna believes that her identity has been challenged in maternity, that her self has been destroyed; her attempts to reconstitute herself involve a distancing from all things maternal. Nevertheless, while Edna's maternal experiences have fractured her sense of self, this is not necessarily the case with Adèle. While the narrator focuses more on Edna's reaction to how changed Adèle is during her labor, Adèle does attempt to control even the last stages of her pregnancy. More specifically, she attempts to control the domestic space in which she is held captive for the duration of labor in her repeated refusals to leave the parlor and go to her bedroom, and she interprets Dr. Mandelet's platitudes about laboring women and the ambivalent attitude of her nurse as hindering an authoring of her own birth experience. Adèle faces significant challenges to securing a sense of authority of experience given how established discourses and social structures attempt to retain control over and condition her subjectivity. Nevertheless, borrowing again from Elaine Orr's theory of negotiation, is it not possible to see Adèle's repeated refusals to confine her pregnant body must be read as an attempt to assemble "a space for influencing the course of change" (13)?

Dr. Mandelet himself warrants further study, for he does not merely represent the stereotypically domineering medical practitioner of the late nineteenth century. Our initial acquaintance with his character is curious in that his advice to Mr. Pontellier with regard to Pontellier's wife, Edna, is superficially chauvinistic. He advises Pontellier to be patient with his way-ward wife, instructing him that all women are "moody" and "whimsical" by nature. Yet even as he passes on the medical establishment's consensus with regard to the "mysterious female," he seems to be speaking these words almost robotically as if he himself were tired of such categorical clichés. In fact, Chopin's initial description of Mandelet is interesting in that she portrays him as more of a "consultant" than a technical expert, who is called upon by those who appreciate his "reputation for wisdom rather than skill" (85). After his conversation with Pontellier, the old doctor doesn't resume the activity of reading that Pontellier interrupts but rather looks "meditatively out at his garden" (88), perhaps questioning his own stereotypical summation of Edna's behavior. Later in the text it is evident that Dr. Mandelet, in his observations of Edna, cultivates a sympathetic understanding of her predicament and might be the only character who senses the threat of her mental state when he says to Edna: "I don't want you to blame yourself, whatever comes" (148). Finally, Dr. Mandelet might be seen as a physician testing the rigid parameters of traditional medicine and seeking to move beyond old stereotypes of women that society has endorsed. Watching Edna witness the birth of Adèle's child essentially forces him to acknowledge that women defy the strict categorization of his teachings and to revise his understand-ing of them in recognizing that they are quite human in their needs and desires. Dr. Mandelet's awakening appears to happen alongside Edna's, and while he ultimately cannot save her in time, we sense that Adèle's next birth (should there be another) will be attended with more concern for her individual needs.

While Adèle does not succeed in transmitting to Edna a "purpose" for the sacrifice and pain that women undergo in pregnancy and childbirth, she does move Edna towards "the vision of a different kind of maternity" that "holds out the possibility of recuperating womanhood, selfhood, society" (Schweitzer 162). And for the first time in women's literature we are forced to interpret the pregnant and birthing body as powerfully explosive in bringing about both creation and potential destruction, perhaps simultaneously. In fact, Adèle forces Edna to recall her own disturbing memories of childbirth which involved "an ecstasy of pain, the heavy odor of chloroform, a stupor which had deadened sensation, an awakening to find a little new life to which she had given being, added to the great unnumbered multitude of souls that come and go" (145). From Chopin's descriptions, it is obvious that Edna's birthing experiences have clearly not been empowering. She is initially stripped of all agency when she is given the chloroform, and upon awakening from the "stupor," she feels not a sense of the miracle of birth but instead a stripping of her individuality. In the multiplication of her own body she has divided herself, and this significantly challenges her understanding of who she is. Though we enter into Adèle's confinement through Edna's eyes and thus it is to be interpreted as restrictive and claustrophobic, Chopin's inclusion of Edna at the birthing scene also allows the reader access to a space that was formerly rarely even referenced. What Tess Chopin offers that is fresh and new is a pregnancy narrative that is wholly unrestricted, complexly detailed, and therefore open to interpretation. Cosslett argues that the "fragmentation of identity involved in the birth process many be horrifying; it may also be enlarging," (142) and Edna's transformation and determination following her witnessing Adèle's childbirth does affect her greatly.

Chopin's intentions with regard to Adèle are about choice—the choice to value the pregnant experience and gain control over it or the choice of a different kind of creative expression; in either case, she offers pregnancy up to her readers as a powerful state of being, as a beautiful and complicated performance. Adèle's motivations for inviting Edna to "witness" her birth experience have widely been explained as an effort to move Edna back to a more domestic sensibility, to urge Edna to "think of the children," and to dismiss any thoughts or acts of transgression. But perhaps Adèle's motivations are more complex. If one looks at the inclusion of Edna into Adèle's experience of pregnancy as an attempt to encourage in Edna something that Adèle herself lacks, we might read this episode entirely differently. Although she herself is confined to the role and perhaps not unhappily so, given her closeness to Edna, she must see that it is not a role meant for her friend. She must know that Edna will react violently to viewing the birth. In fact, Edna's final interaction with

Adèle actually pushes Edna to make the changes in her own life. Adèle's role in the novel is more fundamental to Edna's awakening, then, since it actually coincides with this final interaction with Adèle, and so we see a profound connection between these two women who are attempting to get beyond the masculine restrictions of the times to give birth to their own sense of expression. Cosslett senses such a power in maternal experience when she argues that whether "figured as death or a heroic rebirth, childbirth is, however, always a turning-point, a narrative crisis that destroys, confirms or creates a woman's sense of identity" (154).

Edna's visceral reaction to this "scene of torture," as she calls it, is to flee, to escape any sort of contained domestic space. Adèle is early on exposed as someone who keenly discerns what is underneath the surface in her careful evaluation of Edna and Robert's flirtation, but even in her most heroic efforts to represent the pregnant body as site of power she cannot, because of the restrictive nature of her society, be seen as someone who explodes the term "captive" in a sheer joy in and communion with her body. Such a reading is sorely idealistic; there are too many hints in the narrative to suggest that she actually questions how successful her pregnancies actually are as performances in and of themselves.

Chopin's depictions of all three of her main female characters foreground what Iris Marion Young later articulates, that "to change the experience of [pregnancy and] childbirth means to change women's relationship to fear and powerlessness, to our bodies, to our children" (182). Essentially, Chopin makes her readers aware that when women begin to control their own reproductive abilities, begin to make the choice whether or not to become pregnant, then and only then can pregnancy be fully explored as an experience that might be empowering. Chopin's portrayal of Adèle Ratignolle is sympathetic in her presentation of a thoughtful, loving, intelligent woman undergoing successive pregnancies and, in doing so, attempting to create meaning out of each new pregnancy, struggling with the captivity of the situation, how it affects her life and how others' lives are affected by the choices she has made. It is unfair to conclude that Adèle is merely the stereotypical Madonna figure: the birthing scene reveals her thoughtfulness with regard to her life and to the choices she has made. Importantly, what Chopin does with this pregnancy narrative is disrupt the image that pervaded literature for so long. Adèle is in fact singled out by Chopin for careful characterization in order to present pregnancy as a valid option in woman's struggle towards self-definition, but she is also highlighted to affirm choice, and a woman's choice might not include pregnancy. There is no didacticism in Chopin's text, only a presentation of the realities of pregnancy at the turn of the century. Further, certain aspects of Chopin's pregnancy narrative anticipate questions that women still have regarding authority over the pregnant body. If we gain control of our bodies and begin to understand how the pregnant body intersects with society, can there be more self-awareness? Is Adèle the epitome of the "mother-woman"—someone who has effectively struggled with and won an appreciation of her body as giver of life, as a captive to the needs of others, or does her friendship with Edna suggest her underlying questioning of this choice? Ultimately, the most valuable aspect of this narrative is Edna's interpretation of Adèle's pregnancy and childbirth; that Edna interprets maternity as destructive captivity offers the first dark portrait of pregnancy in American literature and forever alters how writers would interpret "woman's most cherished role."

One of the darkest illustrations of a literary female captive would have to be Charlotte Perkins Gilman's narrator in "The Yellow Wallpaper." Before Chopin included Adèle's pregnancy in the literary canon, Charlotte Perkins Gilman was writing about pregnancy, perhaps indirectly but touching upon it nonetheless. Her short story "The Yellow Wallpaper" not only has become a staple of various anthologies, but it quite literally changed the way that doctors understood and treated post-partum depression. Although the narrator is no longer pregnant in this text, Gilman does suggest that the experience of pregnancy has inaugurated the captivity in which she now lives. The narrator is clearly still inhabiting a captive and sorely misunderstood post-partum body, and the transition from pregnant woman to mother has been impossible for her. Denied the affirmation of pregnancy and childbirth as a monumental transformation in thought and feeling, she is, at the very least, undergoing a dramatic hormonal imbalance that today would be treated with one of many anti-depressants available. Sadly, the narrator is understood only to be a danger to herself and prescribed the infamous "rest-cure" which forbids writing and other creative activities that might actually allow her to work through her feelings of loss and displacement. "The Yellow Wallpaper" was crucial in advancing a conversation, and in 1915 Gilman enriched the discussion once again with regard to how pregnancy has been written into the American landscape with her novel *Herland*.

Herland is quite ahead of its time with regard to its feminist agenda; indeed, its inclusion of a pregnancy narrative is only one of the many ways this text might be explored as a treasure of feminist politics.[6] First published in serialized account in the literary magazine *Forerunner*, *Herland* is Gilman's portrait of a female utopia, told in first-person by Vandyck Jennings, the least offensive of three male characters who accidentally discover and are then taken captive in the utopia Herland. Gilman skillfully chooses a male narrator so that her own voice does not seem to overpower the text, and Jennings therefore recounts the adventures of the men as they are initiated into the all-female and quite progressive society. While two of the three men (including Jennings) become totally taken with their new environment—willing captives, actually—and are impressed with the inhabitants' ideals and accomplishments, there remains a skeptic in the third, Terry, a sexist, brutish guys' guy who has difficulty submitting to the authority of his female captors.

The narrator relates early in the novel that the utopia came about after a cataclysmic event which killed all but a few young women who thereafter claimed the region. Only a few babies were born after the cataclysm, but none survived, and as the narrator tells it, after many years of strengthening the community, one of the women became pregnant without a male partner, through a sort of virgin birth. This same "wonder-woman" bore five girls over the next several years, and after that at the age of twenty-five, each of them bore five daughters, thus engendering a race of women only:

> There you have the start of Herland! One family, all descended
> from one mother! She lived to a hundred years old; lived to see
> her hundred and twenty-five great-granddaughters born; lived
> as Queen-Priestess-Mother of them all; and died with a nobler
> pride and a fuller joy than perhaps any human soul has ever
> known--she alone had founded a new race! (Gilman 59)

Jennings writes of Herland as a land of virtual perfection, where motherhood is considered not only a privilege but also something of a religion. Gilman works against the common notion that to be maternal one must be prototypically feminine in dress and manner like an Adèle Ratignolle. On the contrary, the women of Herland all appear to be middle-aged and not stereotypically feminine and constrained in dress or demeanor, facts which at first shock and rather displease the traveling gentlemen. Gilman sheds light on what Margaret Sanger will likewise highlight in *Motherhood in Bondage*, that in a nation that prides itself on freedom and hope, early twentieth-century America was, in reality, a place determinedly hostile towards pregnancy and motherhood. The irony behind her text is that we must leave America, a place, as Jennings writes, "where mothers are forced to fill and overfill the land, every land, and then see their children suffer, sin, and die" (69), and enter Herland in order to find an environment in which women are glorified and honored for their maternity, a place where "longed-for motherhood was not only a personal joy, but [truly] a nation's hope" (59). Gilman's Herland, as Jennings notes, is a land devoid of strife and inhibition, a place that "included that limitless feeling of sisterhood, that wide unity in service which was so difficult for us to grasp" (69). Interestingly, pregnancy is interpreted by Herland's inhabitants as a rapturous state in which everyone eagerly takes an active supporting role. In fact, Jennings labels them "Conscious Makers of People," for they are determined to nurture both inside the womb and out. The women of Herland define pregnancy as "a child-longing [that grows] within [the woman] until it work[s] its natural miracle" (72). In creating such a safe and empowering environment for the pregnant body, Gilman alludes to the reality of constraint and sometimes oppression which typically defines this condition, suggesting that we must completely restructure society in order to make a positive change. The beliefs she expresses in this novel arguably anticipate later feminist platforms that advocate radical alternatives to traditional male-female procreation. Gilman's novel was written in the early years of the twentieth century, but even so, her enlightened women of Herland have devised a way to populate society without male intervention; it is only when the men penetrate the utopia, marrying the younger women and attempting a new order that traditional procreation becomes a possibility. When Celis becomes pregnant by Jeff (the chivalrous but traditional one of the three male intruders), they are forced to confront this "New Motherhood" (137). Herland's inhabitants have little reservation about the new motherhood because of their sincere elevation of the maternal state, and they perhaps naively see such a union as another way to enrich their knowledge. Jennings characterizes Celis' revelation of her pregnancy as a rebirth: "Celis, her blue eyes swimming in happy tears, her heart lifted with that tide of race-motherhood which was her supreme passion, could with ineffable joy and pride announce that she was to be a mother" (137). Her news is received well by the other women, who cloak her in a robe of affection, adoration, projecting onto her "breathless reverence," Gilman writes, like those who "watched the miracle of virgin birth [with] deep awe and warm expectancy" (138). This "approach to motherhood" creates a sacred time when love and longing have reached their apex. The reader, however, recognizes that with the intrusion of the men this ideal society will be forever altered. Gilman, perhaps unintentionally, anticipates the intermingling of technology with the pregnant and birthing body when she presents her reader with a race of women who produce only female children and without male intervention. Though she couches her narrative in a mystical fashion, this scientific or magical feat forces us to think about how women might interpret the experiences of pregnancy and childbirth if given sole authorship of these experiences. What she paints is a glorious portrait of the body in a captivated rather than captive state, free from restrictions and prescriptions, but there remains a cautious awareness of how such harmony will forever be threatened by those who desire to use it for their own ends—here the men who infiltrate Herland, symbolizing, in turn, the establishment that seeks to name, decipher, limit, and further subjugate the female body. Gilman is here a writer interested in highlighting in the palimpsestic subtext of her utopia the various ways that women's bodies and minds have been compromised by edicts that pretend to offer assistance and comfort.

Edith Wharton is perhaps best known for the biting wit she employs to critique upper-class New Yorkers and their frivolous and destructive habits; she is perhaps technically superior to Gilman in elaborating a subtle critique of social habits and behaviors that are taken for granted as safe or beneficial. According to critic Dale M. Bauer, Wharton's later fictions address "the politics of intimate experience in the context of social debates" (49). Tess Cosslett notes in *Women Writing Childbirth*, "a 'medicalized' version of childbirth, in which women are objectified as machines for producing babies, has become increasingly dominant in the twentieth century" (2), and further argues that such treatment strips women of subjectivity with regard to childbirth. While ostensibly the established medical community has tended to promote the epidural and the cesarean as the safest options (in 2002 more than one-fourth of first-time mothers delivered their infants via cesarean), Cosslett argues that through analgesia women may be robbed of subjectivity with regard to childbirth. Wharton's 1927 novel *Twilight Sleep* reveals in its title an interest in how newly emerging medical interventions intersect with the upper-crust New York female pregnant and birthing body. Wharton includes a subtext about pregnancy early in her novel meant to fuel discussion about methods of pain alleviation that were beginning in the late 1920's to change a woman's birthing experience. In her 1992 work *The American Way of Birth*, Jessica Mitford historicizes the growth of the twilight sleep phenomenon, citing that after numerous rich American women traveled to Germany to partake of the drug during delivery, there grew swiftly a demand for twilight sleep in the States, the treatment becoming "the anaesthetic of choice, routinely administered in the more go-ahead hospitals along the Eastern seaboard" (53). Most interesting and disturbing are the ingredients of twilight sleep, which, according to Mitford are "akin to those used in the 'truth serum' we read about in sensational accounts of interrogations of prisoners of war and other captives at the mercy of their jailors" (53).[7] Furthermore, as

Bauer notes in her "Twilight Sleep: Edith Wharton's Brave New Politics," the twilight sleep method was available only to upper class women, so 'gaining power'… was class power"(57). Essentially these women "lose power over their bodies in sleeping through childbirth, and they disassociate themselves from lower class 'robust' women" at the same time (57). Bauer sees Wharton using her power as a literary heavyweight not only to critique and interrogate the twilight sleep movement but also the eugenics movement "she likened in 1925 to the 'long arm of the Inquisition'" (58). Mitford's research reveals that there is consensus that the labor and delivery experiences were anything but serene under the power of twilight sleep. In fact, most women, she writes, "report[ed] hazy memories of having felt like an animal howling in pain" (55). Perhaps most disturbing is Mitford's claim that obstetricians favored this drug due to the control that it gave them over their patients undergoing labor and delivery. Although Wharton would not have known that twilight sleep would later be condemned by the scientific community as unsafe to mother and child and largely abandoned before World War II, she at least seems to sense there is something profoundly disturbing in the cultish following that it enjoys in her own era and what it means to the experience of childbirth and motherhood.[8]

Mitford's historical grounding of the twilight sleep movement lends the contemporary reader a different lens through which to analyze Wharton's interest in the repercussions of this "anaesthetic panacea" in her own novel *Twilight Sleep*. As is the case with many of the early narratives highlighting the pregnant body, Wharton's focus is directed at a rather peripheral character. In her novel Wharton introduces Lita Wyant, daughter-in-law of the text's focal character Pauline Manford, a young woman characterized as the stereotypical mindless socialite whose "every moment … was crammed with dancing, riding, and games" (17). There is very little evidence to suggest that Lita ponders the philosophical ramifications of her own pregnancy; rather, the narrator relates, she "had sunk into a state of smiling animal patience, as the mysterious work going on in her tender young body had a sacred significance for her, and it was enough to lie still and let it happen" (18). With regard to her pregnancy, "all she asked was that nothing should 'hurt' her: she had the blind dread of physical pain common also to most of the young women of her set" (18). Physical pain, Wharton relates through the voice of Pauline (a woman who constantly seeks the newest "remedy"), has been virtually eliminated in the upper classes with the invention of twilight sleep, thus allowing Lita to experience childbirth "as lightly and unperceivingly as if the wax doll which suddenly appeared in the cradle at her bedside had been brought there in one of the big bunches of hot-house roses that she found every morning on her pillow" (18).

Pauline describes pregnancy and childbirth as somehow detached from real experience: "'Of course there ought to be no Pain....[,] nothing but Beauty.... It ought to be one of the loveliest, most poetic things in the world to have a baby'" (18). Wharton's skepticism becomes clear when she exposes Pauline as one who views babies as "something to be turned out in series like Fords" (18). Despite their superficialities, both Pauline and Lita exhibit dissatisfaction with the atmosphere in which they reside. Although they are granted every material comfort and extravagance, they are constantly seeking the next best activity or recreation. Pauline, in fact, wears her "causes" as she might a new jacket; in one comical scene she delivers a speech to a "Mother's Group" using the opening lines of her "Birth Control" speech: "No more effaced wives, no more drudging mothers, no more human slaves crushed by the eternal round of housekeeping and child-bearing" (97). This is, however, only a paradoxical opening, used in order to frame her speech for the group of mothers who comprise her audience on that particular day: "That's what our antagonists say—the women who are afraid to be mothers, the women who put their enjoyment and their convenience and what they call their happiness before the mysterious heaven-sent joy, the glorious privilege, of bringing children into the world—"(98). While we remain unclear as to Pauline's views on the subject of child-bearing and motherhood, these contradictory stances suggest that she is desperately searching for an understanding of herself in a society that pretends to offer self definition for women but rarely delivers. Pauline's ability to speak as an advocate for the mothers' group one moment and then the birth control movement the next reflects her desire to advocate for something, just unsure as to what might offer her the most hope of the power to define herself and her voice. Like the choice between natural childbirth or childbirth with pain alleviation, there is no clear understanding of what experience—"embracing" the pain or "controlling" the pain—will be more empowering. Lita, like Pauline, in flitting from one unfulfilling activity to the next is not actually frivolous but, rather, looking for something worthwhile on which to focus her substantial energies. In fact, both Pauline's daughter Nona, and Pauline's husband Dexter Manford notice that Lita seems "restless, [and] vaguely impatient with things," always pursuing new "frauds and flatterers" (107). She has, after all, been encouraged to "sleep" through any experiences that might enrich her both emotionally and intellectually, and in doing so she has become frustrated and limited.

Still, Wharton's conclusion seems to be that Lita Wyant's true captivity rests in both her willful ignorance in allowing the mystery of pregnancy and childbirth to be taken out of her hands by those who believe they know better, and this critique clearly entails frustration at a medical establishment that advocates an emotional and philosophical retreat from consideration of such a valuable life experience. Critic Helena Michie evokes Paul Morrison's concept of the "domestic carceral" in her analysis of her own pregnancy in her article entitled "Confinements: The Domestic in the Discourses of Upper-Middle-Class Pregnancy," Michie recalls how in her seventh month of pregnancy she joined in the inevitable tour of the labor and delivery room and encountered a space that is attempting to capture the feeling of "home." Not only did this space fail to provide Michie with a sense of comfort, she found these "birthing suites" disturbing in their obvious attempts to "offer the promise of safety, domesticity, and control" (59). Beneath the benign surface is a space "filled with the gothic apparatus of medicine" (58). In fact, with the push of one button, the room becomes, according to Michie, "an operating room oddly crowded with remnants from the showroom of Ethan Allen" (59). Michie's profound discomfort derives from her feelings of powerlessness with regard to her experience of childbirth. The room looks like home or at least some version of home, but in one instant, it transforms into a prison-like space, attempting to limit her both physically and psychically.

Lita's birthing room, similarly, as full of hothouse flowers and as reminiscent of home as it might be, actually serves to reinforce how women of her class are discouraged from considering pregnancy and childbirth as complicated but potentially enriching experiences and, rather, encouraged to detach themselves from these experiences altogether. The fact that Wharton chooses to name her novel after a drug that then becomes a metaphor for the imposed restriction and enforced compliance that a woman might experience with regard to pregnancy, labor, and childbirth moves her into a space occupied by the other writers discussed in this chapter. Therefore, she joins the discussion as to how women might become best able to captivate themselves with the pregnant and birthing body rather than allowing themselves to become captives to an establishment that seeks to dilute, redirect, or define the experience for them. Wharton indirectly scorns a culture that allows this to happen and scolds a culture for "sleeping" through and retreating from a consideration of pregnancy and childbirth. Wharton's characters believe themselves to be achieving control over their bodies through pain alleviation, but she argues forcefully through the machinations of plot that in alleviating pain they are actually detaching themselves from lived experience.

While the caustic wit of Wharton's social critiques allows the reader to remain somewhat unemotional and detached from the issues she tackles, the humor of Flannery O'Connor's most famous stories like "Good Country People" and "A Good Man is Hard to Find" has almost completely the opposite effect. In fact, it almost always touches a nerve that makes it viscerally felt. Such a reaction is almost impossible to avoid with regard to O'Connor's less famous 1949 story "A Stroke of Good Fortune." Unlike the upper-class, beautiful, and ethereal Lita Wyant, O'Connor's protagonist Ruby Hill is a lower-to-middle class woman, "a short woman, shaped nearly like a funeral urn," (95) whose life is predictably average; indeed, our introduction to Ruby is of her returning from the store, overheated, exhausted, unkempt, with hair "stacked in sausage rolls around her head...loose with the heat and [from] the long walk" (95). In this story O'Connor brings the topic of pregnancy into the discourse of regular people, and though this particular piece may be familiar to the contemporary reader in its candor with regard to the condition of pregnancy, the reader must be reminded of the atmosphere in which O'Connor was writing—on the cusp of a decade remembered for its dedication to "family values." Rosemary Betterton's article entitled "Prima Gravida" focuses on visual art that disrupts the "ideological norms of the feminine and the maternal as a result of differently imag-ined or experienced body schema" (266) in an attempt to counter the historical representations of the pregnant body, as either "container for another being or as subjected to a process that is beyond her control" (266). Betterton's frustration that "neither model pays attention to the embodied viewpoint of the maternal subject nor to pregnancy as a process in itself" (266) can be extended toward literary images of pregnancy as well. Shocking in its candor and unapologetic in its willingness to defy the norm, Flannery O'Connor's work challenges the safe evasions of experience that many choose to inhabit. O'Connor chooses words rather than paintbrush or chisel, but the end result would most likely please Betterton's sensibilities. O'Connor rejects any model of pregnancy that precedes her in her brutally honest treatment of the emotions a woman might experience when she learns her body has been taken captive, quite literally, by another being.

As readers, we are aware from the outset of the story that Ruby Hill is indeed pregnant, though we are forced to muddle through her denials of the truth and to join in the pain of her eventual recognition. Ruby's invocations of pregnancy are startlingly negative in that they call to mind recollections of her unfortunate mother, a woman she describes as "a puckered up old yellow apple" who "had always looked like she wasn't satisfied with anything" (95). What she has seen with regard to her own mother's pregnancies is only a world of despair, stunted hope, and ruined possibility, and how "her mother had got deader with every one of them" (97). Ruby's estrangement from her own body is pronounced; in fact, it is not until her neighbor, Laverne Watts, deciphers her condition that Ruby starts to read her body realistically. O'Connor hints at Ruby's distance from her body in the opening page of the story when she describes how Ruby "gazed with stony unrecognition at the face that confronted her in the dark yellow-spotted mirror" (95). Throughout the story we witness a breakdown in Ruby's attempts to control her appearance, from her unawareness of the "gritty collard leaf" stuck to her face to her awareness of the tightness of her only "loose" skirt. Pregnancy, for Ruby, is a sentence like that of cancer, for it represents an invasion and a loss of bodily integrity and control. In fact, she would prefer to learn that she suffers from heart trouble because, as she puts it, "they couldn't very well remove your heart" (99). Ruby is determined to keep her bodily integrity intact, and, in her mind, pregnancy initiates a violation of this integrity whereby the fetus takes what it needs from the mother in a Gothic fashion.[9] Critic Claire Kahane sees O'Connor as preoccupied with studying a woman's own "fascination with the hidden processes of her body, a fascination no doubt intensified by [her] own mysterious and debilitating illness" (247).

Ruby has seen in her mother and sisters' pregnancies a gradual loss of self, an eating away of possibility, and her denial of the possibility of pregnancy is in part an effect of her interpretation of pregnancy as a violation of her independent motivations and desires. Further, since she views herself as the only member of her family with any "get," she believes the acceptance of her condition to be a forced recognition of a shared commonality with those she pities. Unlike Wharton, O'Connor allows her readers thorough engagement with Ruby's thoughts, and in doing so Ruby is able to communicate how offensive she finds pregnant bodies. Even as she forcefully denies the possibility of pregnancy, Ruby begins to feel "the wholeness of herself, a whole thing climbing the stairs" (99). It is crucial for Ruby to feel such wholeness, to feel herself in control of her physical body. In fact, retaining such control allows her to feel at the helm of her own narrative. Again, underlying Ruby's own narrative is her mother's—read as something of a story of the poor woman's Adèle Ratignolle, neither honored nor praised for her sacrifices. In fact, we only hear Ruby's mother's story secondhand, for this woman is not granted a place in O'Connor's narrative. Consequently, her silence is the more compelling than if she held a prominent place in the narrative because such silence demonstrates how she has been held forever captive by her own procreative experiences. Enduring her multitude pregnancies, Ruby's mother has all her own agency erased, and Ruby would rather be the victim of a heart condition than face such a fate.

Ruby, not surprisingly, interprets her lack of fecundity as a blessing. In fact, she regards every passing year without a pregnancy to be a sort of triumph over what she views as a powerful force pressing unwanted responsibility on her. She wants to believe Madame Zoleeda's prediction that the long illness she will face will be one that ends in a "stroke of good fortune." Since neither pregnancy nor motherhood strikes Ruby as good fortune, she hangs onto Madame Zoleeda's prophesy as her guarantee of non-pregnancy. Ruby's own previous experience dealing with childbirth is restricted to that of being present at her brother Rufus's birth, and she reacts to Rufus's birthing scene in much the same fashion that Edna Pontellier responds to Adèle Ratignolle's. She reads it as a scene of torture and tries to escape by going to three successive movies, but the ferocity of the labor is still going strong when she returns, and so she must endure the screams all night. Ruby's response to her mother's sacrifice is to exclaim, "All that misery for Rufus" (97), Rufus's existence inadequate compensation for such pain and agony. Much as Edna views the birth of her children to be a sort of countdown to her own demise, when Ruby as a child looks at her pregnant mother, all she sees is an unborn child "waiting to make his mother, only thirty-four, into an old woman" (97).

As the above quote foregrounds, O'Connor's text explores the American woman's fear that pregnancy and motherhood will incite the aging process. Ruby recalls how her mother, at thirty-four, has grey hair and wrinkled skin, so, therefore, is less attractive in Ruby's eyes. She herself, in avoiding numerous pregnancies, continuously emphasizes her youthful appearance. She believes her mother got "a little deader" (97) with every pregnancy, a little less attractive, more puckered and undesirable. As she continues to reject the possibility of pregnancy, she keeps exhorting herself to be "warm and fat and beautiful," not "dried up" (99) like her mother. The aging process itself is particularly reviled in this piece, as becomes evident in Ruby's description of her older neighbor, Mr. Jerger, whom Ruby describes as resembling a goat with a face that "looked as if it had mildew on it" (99). Ruby's belief is that pregnancy triggers the aging process to begin its rapid conquest of the body and mind, and she is mentally held captive by the representations of the experience that she has witnessed around her, unable to create a new context for her own experience of pregnancy. Interestingly, O'Connor invokes in Ruby's fear of doctors the control of traditional medicine in the reproductive lives of the women by whom she is surrounded. Ruby, believing herself to have more sense than her mother or sisters proudly states, "I kept myself away from doctors all my life" (103), implicitly arguing that the doctors who have attended her relatives have had an agenda of their own. She views the condition of pregnancy to be relinquishing oneself willingly to a threatening establishment and wonders how her sisters suffer their fate of "always going to the doctor to be jabbed at with instruments" (97).

Although Ruby exhibits moments of insight, she is not an intelligent woman, and although she may have more "get" than others in her family, she is unable to reenvision her own pregnancy as anything other than captivity in the worst possible sense. O'Connor's portrayal is illuminating in many ways. The repulsion that Ruby feels toward pregnant bodies is dramatic; few have had the audacity to write of pregnancy in this manner. O'Connor's depiction, although devastating, allows the reader into the mind of the pregnant woman who is attempting to decipher how dramatically this experience will change her life. When Ruby's neighbor, Laverne, recognizes Ruby's condition and verbalizes it, Ruby vehemently rejects this linguistic "prodding" of a body that she has thus far kept in her control. When Laverne notices that it is "not just [Ruby's] ankles" that are swollen but that "[Ruby's] swollen all over" (105), Ruby seeks to silence her as if the verbalization of her condition will make it a reality. Ruby responds by saying, "I ain't going to stay here and be insulted," and she moves toward the door "keeping herself erect and not looking down at her stomach" (105). In fact, Laverne never actually uses the word "pregnancy" to describe Ruby's condition, so Ruby is still able mentally to settle on her condition as that of "heart trouble," a fate preferable to the alternative. There is no contrived acceptance of fate resulting in satisfaction in her new experience. Even in the last pages of the story Ruby condemns the being inside her as one "waiting in her to make her deader" (106).

With candor and unapologetic force, O'Connor moves a study of pregnancy to a primary position—here an experience that obviously impacts women's lives, their perceptions of themselves and society. As critic Robin May Schott argues, "it remains historically true that the events of menstruation, pregnancy, childbirth, and menopause form significant junctures in women's lives, with varying degrees of intensity. To delegitimate reflection on this sphere of human existence is to reiterate the categories of masculine thought that postmodernism ostensibly seeks to deconstruct" (175). Some critics suggest that O'Connor thrusts Ruby into this experience as representing a universal experience of confronting what most horrifies you. Is this story also to be read as a particular warning to women to avoid pregnancy in order to retain control of their own "narratives?" There is danger in reducing O'Connor's story to such a cautionary tale. Is there anything hopeful in O'Connor's presentation of pregnancy? The hopefulness lies in the fact that she includes such a vivid depiction of the body, rejecting classic models and allowing for more revisions, which do come later, especially in the texts of African American women writers. In order to work through how we might reimagine the imposed captivity of pregnancy as a captivating and enlightening experience, it is imperative that we understand the devastation that pregnancy has historically wrought on the female body, and O'Connor's story helps us gain this understanding.

Flannery O'Connor's story anticipates a number of writings that follow, especially with regard to working class and African American writers, whose depictions of pregnancy are always couched in terms of the hardships of class and race. Ruby Hill is no mother-woman, and in creating her, O'Connor continues in the tradition of Chopin, illustrating how certain women question pregnancy as the only way to achieve true "womanhood." What separates O'Connor's depiction from the rest of the fold is her refusal to blame Ruby's distaste for pregnancy on a compromised economic or racial factor. Ruby is merely a bold portrayal of a woman trying to control her own body, trying to prevent what she views as a devastating destiny, which includes a loss of independent movement and thought. Ruby's character is not by any means sympathetic. Clearly, she is not the prototypical nurturing female that has pervaded literature over the centuries, nor is she particularly clever or ambitious. O'Connor creates her to be average as if to say that even the most average (perhaps especially the average) do not have to accept a destiny that was long ago decided upon by an established or privileged sector of the population. O'Connor's Ruby Hill cannot even begin to understand how the pregnant form might be a potential site of power or control because the pregnant body has been so unfavorably inscribed in her particular society. Even though the ending suggests Ruby must confront what she experiences as anything but "a stroke of good fortune," O'Connor's story also reads as an important turning-point in a body of literature aimed at reclaiming the experiences of pregnancy and childbirth away from patriarchal control.

The works discussed in this chapter are varied in their concerns with regard to the pregnant and birthing body. Gilman and Wharton are more focused on the social and political implications of pregnancy on the female body, while Chopin and O'Connor seem more interested in bringing these subjects into the literature of their respective times as a way perhaps to challenge ideas about which life experiences are worthy of scholarly or critical thought. What unifies these authors, besides the similar acclaim they have ultimately enjoyed as we look back at literature of the twentieth century, is that they are all interested in the ways that the experiences of pregnancy and childbirth might be transformed through a possible reenvisioning of the language used to describe them and through a reinterpretation of the captive state in general. What radiates from their respective writings is how these women writers were all drawn to the possibility of true authority over experience, to the elusive reality of defining pregnancy and childbirth as not merely interesting subject matter but also as a female-authored and female-defined experience. The following chapter, though concentrated on the era of the Depression, reveals the ways that writers of this period use the pregnant and birthing body as a way into the discourse of the times and as a means of further differentiating the female voice from the male voice in working-class literature.

Notes

[1]From *Misconceptions*, p.9

[2]Chopin's short story "Athénaïse" is often read as a story of a woman's total welcoming of the experience of pregnancy and motherhood. Michael Lund suggests "'Athénaïse' must also be seen as just one of Chopin's many explorations of female identity in the nineteenth century (102). Moreover, critic Patricia Hopkins Lattin adds that "Athénaïse's feeling complete because of her pregnancy" is a reaction "based on momentary emotion rather than experience" (9).

[3]For instance, Ivy Schweitzer, in her "Maternal Discourse and the Romance of Self-Possession in Kate Chopin's *The Awakening*," is one of many critics who have little use for Adèle Ratignolle, regarding her as "a surface of clichés, easily accessible as the fulfillment of romantic 'dreams' in which we all take refuge from 'reality'" (169). Though Schweitzer sees Edna as a woman aware of how maternity is the "introduction to a double alienation" (169), she does not see Adèle as one who realizes how her desire has been compromised by domesticity.

[4]Dr. Naphey also suggested that a woman not stand or kneel for long periods, "nor sing in either of these postures." He furthermore recommends that "those who have not been accustomed to bathing should not

begin this practice during pregnancy" (Bailey 254).

[5]As Jennifer Mather Saul points out in her 2003 book *Feminism: Issues and Arguments*, Betty Friedan and her contemporaries "focused on the importance of women moving into the labor force," distancing themselves from maternal issues (31). Tellingly, the word "pregnancy" does not even appear in the index of this newly published text as if to underscore the irrelevance of the experience to feminist pursuits.

[6]According to Deborah Madsen in *Feminist Theory and Literary Practice*, Gilman's feminist agenda included an emphasis "upon reform of the existing economic structure to open up equal opportunities for women by freeing them from restrictive inherited gender roles" (43). Gilman's perception was that under a capitalist patriarchy women must please men in order to survive and therefore have no realistic alternative for themselves.

[7]According to Mitford, twilight sleep was actually "hypodermic injections of morphine combined with scopalomine (a powerful hallucinogenic and amnesiac) and pentobarbital sodium ... given every hour" (53). While some feminists believed this concoction to be a way for women to gain more control over nature and the "inevitable" pain of labor and delivery, Mitford counters such a hope with several negative examples of reactions women had to twilight sleep based on documentation by those present at delivery.

[8]Though twilight sleep was largely abandoned as a pain alleviation method in most parts after World War II, Mitford disturbingly recounts that in some regions of the country twilight sleep was used until 1974.

[9]For further discussion of Ruby's pregnancy as Gothic experience, see Claire Kahane's article "The Maternal Legacy: The Grotesque Tradition in Flannery O'Connor's Female Gothic," in *The Female Gothic*, ed. Juliann E. Fleenor. London: Eden Press, 1983.

CHAPTER 3

WORKING-CLASS WRITERS ON PREGNANCY: FREEING THE SOCIALLY/ECONOMICALLY CAPTIVE BODY

> Woman must write herself: must write about women and bring women to writing, from which they have been driven away as violently as from their bodies—for the same reasons, by the same law, with the same fatal goal. Woman must put herself into the text—as into the world and into history—by her own movement. —Hélène Cixous[1]

James L. Murphy argues in *The Proletarian Moment* that the discussion over leftism "remains relevant and merits reexamination" given that the issues addressed are still pertinent today, especially with regard to "the specific nature and function of creative literature; and the relation between art and politics [and between] literature and propaganda" (3). Murphy further emphasizes the need to study a literature that was born of a particular moment by referring to how this literary movement "was pervasive in the cultural life of the thirties" (3). However, though Murphy refers to some of the most noteworthy male writers in American working-class literature, he omits important female writers of the same era whose work should be reexamined as some of the most revelatory literature of this particular historical era in America. Certainly the name Meridel Le Sueur does not evoke a movement as does the name Michael Gold. Indeed, according to Murphy, "no name is more closely connected with the proletarian literature movement in the United States than Gold's" (64).[2] Regardless of his stature as a working-class writer, Michael Gold has been heavily criticized by feminist scholars for the way that he leaves little room for a female presence within his own writing. After all, Gold hardly invites the female writer to join in when he characterizes the proletarian writer in "Go Left" as a "wild" working-class youth who "works in the lumber camps, coal mines, steel mills, harvest fields and mountain camps of America" (4).

In sharp contrast, female working-class writing is distinguishable from male working-class writing in its efforts to convey the oftentimes painful but potentially evocative nature and captivating qualities of maternity, along with other specifically female experiences. Sadly, though, the female experience has often been relegated to the margins. According to Shelley Fisher Fishkin in her introduction to Tillie Olsen's *Silences*, it was not until the 1970s, and after the appearance of Olsen's influential book, that the Feminist Press began publishing the works of a number of women writers like Le Sueur, Fielding Burke, Tess Slesinger, and many others whose work had been all but forgotten. Despite this critical forgetfulness, we can now see that writing of the distinctly female experiences of pregnancy and childbirth became a way for working-class women writers to distinguish themselves—effectively creating a subgenre of literature that was meant to reinforce their right to a place in a literary history that for so long was reserved only for male voices. A shared characteristic of the work of Margaret Sanger, Le Sueur, and Olsen is, according to critic Joanne Frye, "a commitment to writing about ordinary human experiences, particularly those of women and of working-class people" (3), though their writings of the very human (and female) experiences of pregnancy and childbirth are decidedly different. Margaret Sanger chooses merely to frame real women's stories, and in doing so ignites a political firestorm, and while Tillie Olsen's response wants to affirm the experience but does not explain it, Meridel Le Sueur is determined to document pregnancy as a beneficially transcendent experience. This chapter focuses on Sanger's *Motherhood in Bondage*, Olsen's *Yonnondio: From the Thirties* and *Silences*, and Le Sueur's "Annunciation" and *The Girl* so as to reveal how pregnancy and childbirth were written into working-class literature, thus defining and legitimizing female experience amidst one of America's most trying economic and social disruptions.

Toril Moi argues in *Sexual/Textual Politics* that "women are central—not marginal—to the process of reproduction"; she further argues that "it is precisely because the ruling order cannot maintain the status quo without the continued exploitation and oppression of [working class women] that it seeks to mask their central economic role by marginalizing them on the cultural, ideological and political levels" (171). The motivation behind Margaret Sanger's *Motherhood in Bondage*, published in 1929, reflects Moi's concern that the "paradox of the position of women and the working class is that they are at one and the same time central and marginal(ized)" (171). Born on September 14, 1879, in New York, Sanger's own personal history seems to have motivated the path that she would pave in championing women's reproductive health issues. In fact, Sanger points to her mother's frequent pregnancies as the underlying cause of the latter's death. Fueled by frustration at the lack of control women had over their own reproductive health, she entered the White Plains Hospital nursing program in 1900 and thereafter worked in New York's Lower East Side with poor women suffering the pains of frequent childbirth, miscarriage, and abortion. It was during such visits that Sanger realized the captivity in which these women lived. Not only were they often physically abused by husbands and lovers who had no regard for the toll numerous pregnancies had on these women's bodies, but they were likewise denied access to any means of birth control that might allow them certain corporeal freedoms. Obviously, Sanger is well-known for her accomplishments as a social activist and reformer, but her personal involvement with the very women for whom she advocates in her many speeches and pamphlets speaks to the genuine interest she had for the actual lives she champions in her causes.[3]

Motherhood in Bondage can only be described as a documentary of devastation, a bombardment of individual letters written to Sanger by women who look to her as their own personal savior in a political crusade for women's reproductive health rights. Stories predominate of women too tired and financially challenged to handle the children they have, too weak to endure another pregnancy and childbirth, and completely at a loss as to how to improve their situations. This collection of letters, and Sanger's own analysis of the imposed captivity of poverty-stricken and desperate women responding to unwanted pregnancies, is her own political statement and, as she argues in her introduction, a strong testament to the poor American woman's lack of control over her own childbearing body.[4] Sanger frames each section of her book with her own commentary, but the actual letters are so powerful that she really had no need to emphasize them; in fact, the letters work well together to portray pregnancy as a death sentence and birth control as an elusive panacea. Clearly the impetus behind the publication of these letters is Sanger's desire to focus women's health issues more on the actual lives of women and not on the vague statistics that ultimately prove useless in deciding the fate of the childbearing body. What is in reality only a collection of letters becomes an agonizing litany of desperation, illustrating how poverty lends itself to captivity of the mind and body.

To speak of pregnancy as an empowering experience seems pointless if not frivolous with regard to the lives of the women in these letters. Sanger herself realized that "if [a woman's] past experience in bringing children into the world has been one of suffering and of a kind to strike terror to her heart, the mother is forced into a situation in which she is ready to accept the only way out—abortion" (Sanger 394). It is punishing to a woman who was (and a reader who is) able to enjoy her childbearing body to recognize the emotional and social captivity these women endured. For example, we must read the following empathetically: "During pregnancy I nearly died with hard fits" (73); "I am so afraid of becoming pregnant" (85); "I am so rundown from childbirth" (85); [I've] been to the asylum once on account of childbirth" (93); "[I'm] in constant fear of becoming pregnant again" (105); "Oh, the awful worry of getting pregnant" (131); "My uterus is badly torn, dropped and fallen backwards against my rectum" (143). To be sure, it is almost impossible to turn to a page within the text in which fear and pain are not the pervasive emotions. Perhaps most disturbing is the overall apologetic tone of these letters; moreover, it is obvious that these women are not embellishing but instead downplaying the extent of their discomfort. Had these women not written to Sanger, documenting their experiences of pregnancy, childbirth, and motherhood, I certainly would not have had the luxury to write about pregnancy as one experience in which a woman might be comfortable enough physically actually to begin to work through the mind/body conflict to achieve a sense of power. The women whose lives are documented in Sanger's book may not be privileged enough ever to know how their own maternity might empower them, but their stories do reveal a starting point in recorded responses to issues of pregnancy and childbirth. It is through shining a light on their captivity that we begin perhaps to understand further the complexities of the pregnant and childbearing body, for, in these published pleas for solutions to incessant pregnancies and childbirths, women's bodies are pushed to the forefront of the political stage.

Sanger, along with her husband William Sanger, was a part of a circle of intellectuals, activists, and artists (Upton Sinclair among them), and she, like her comrades, was not one to shy away from a political challenge. It is apparent within the pages of *Motherhood in Bondage* that Sanger knew her audience and crafted her book accordingly. She effectively uses several clever rhetorical strategies in order to move her middle-to-upper-class audience to see how "girl-wives, burdened with premature pregnancies and childbirths, are dragged down ... [and] made prematurely old by the clash of instincts and environments over which they have no control" (intro l). Sanger further argues that in distancing themselves from this reality, the privileged few are "countenancing a type of slavery that is a disgrace to American ideals and that constitution which guarantees to every citizen the right to life, liberty and the pursuit of happiness" (intro liii). Sanger's introduction works well to humanize the nameless, faceless women who permeate her text, arguing that "despite their limitations, their lack of education, these mothers reveal themselves strangely conscious of their duty to the race, of the sacredness of their maternal function" (intro li). Later, in the body of the text, she effectively gives order to what might initially appear chaotic by organizing the letters into headings like "Girl Mothers," "The Trap of Maternity," "The Struggle of the Unfit," "The Sins of the Fathers," "Double Slavery," "Voices of the Children," and "Solitary Confinement." Using words like "struggle," "sins," and "slavery," she continues the argument that Charlotte Perkins Gilman makes in *Herland* that all Americans are culpable for the devastating conditions in which these poor women live.

What the contemporary reader is immediately struck by is the repetition of the pleas within the letters, though in Sanger's careful organization she refuses to allow the reader distance by highlighting the numerous problems to be addressed, emphasizing that this is a highly complicated and multi-layered struggle. Furthermore, Sanger introduces each section of her book with a pointed argument for change to this or that situation. For instance, her introduction for "The Struggle of the Unfit" is strategic in its argument that while "there is a certain class of women predestined by Nature to the high calling of motherhood, it is no less evident that there are others completely unfit for it" (60). While it is obvious that Sanger believes that birth control should be made available to all women, and that all women, regardless of their fortitude or position in society, should be granted a choice, she appeals in this section to those who need empirical evidence why some should be exempted from repeated and unwanted pregnancies. Indeed, "The Struggle of the Unfit" is a torturous description of complications, physical and mental ordeals, and the "feeble struggle for life in an environment which must doom [both the mother and child] from the start" (61).

Though her featured women are poor and have few choices, Sanger uses her own position in society to guarantee that their voices are heard. She is not a working-class writer in the same sense that the other writers featured here are given that she was born into relative wealth and security. Nevertheless, her dedication to the working-class cause is unmistakable. In these women's lives, Sanger argues, poverty and maternity have been irrevocably intertwined. Her argument underscores the obvious: that it is in America's best interest to improve the lives of these women, that "poverty multiplied by ignorance, hunger, disease, congenital defect, cannot be a proper breeding-ground for the future generations of America" (25). Couching her argument in "what is best for America" is a political attention-grabber, and while the letters are strikingly similar in content, including the phrases "I am a poor woman" (27), "My mother died at childbirth and I had to take care [of her children]. She had fifteen children. I don't want any for awhile" (194), "It seems I can't keep out of the family way" (223), "In the last eight [years] I have given birth to two stillborn children, one living one, and have miscarried four times, making seven times in the eight years I have been pregnant" (139), Sanger uses each story as both a highly individual and a unremittingly shameful representation of America's refusal to champion women's health and reproductive rights. Sanger's role as a writer and activist was merely to illuminate the problem and to provide the appropriate social platform to enact change by both highlighting and condemning the lack of authority that these women have over their own bodies, but her efforts had more of an effect than perhaps even she imagined. Even today, in an America that ostensibly grants women ample freedom with regard to maternity, the fears and concerns reflected in the voices in these letters do not sound as remote as they should. A poor pregnant woman is still held captive in various ways—captive to a healthcare system that favors the rich and captive to a medical establishment that often discourages authority and choice. Sanger revealed in the publication of *Motherhood in Bondage* that her featured women were indeed held captive by a system that continuously failed them. Almost seventy-five years later, women are still struggling to gain control of the pregnant and childbearing body, so perhaps a return to Sanger's book is both timely and necessary in order to see how far we *have not* come.

While Margaret Sanger's own life did not mirror those she serves as advocate for in *Motherhood in Bondage*, Tillie Olsen's work is without a doubt a reflection of her own personal involvement and shared experience in the lives of the working-class women of whom she writes. Olsen writes in direct response to the aftermath of the Great Depression, and her involvement in the leftist political movement allowed her to voice her opinions, even if women's issues were sometimes subordinated to other issues, more obviously driven by economics. Critics Alice Kessler-Harris and Paul Lauter argue in their introduction to Murphy's *The Proletarian Moment* that the Leftist movement was important in giving authority to the female voice on various issues, and while "the nature of women's participation in political action limited the issues about which they wrote, it also provided depth and insight into the critical, social, and personal conflicts that underlay activism" (xi). Nevertheless, certain issues that were crucial to women's lives were silenced by stronger voices, like Michael Gold's.[5] Kessler-Harris and Lauter point out that "in denying the commonalities of female experience, the vision of the proletarian aesthetic undermined such crucial issues for women as the uneven division of household labor, the sexual double standard, and male chauvinism within the working class" (intro xi). Olsen's *Silences*, in contrast, acknowledges and reflects upon the hardships that women face in their attempts to combine both maternity and the working world. In *Three Radical Women Writers*, Nora Ruth Roberts significantly details the circumstances of Olsen's own life and growth as a socialist advocate.[6] Roberts reiterates Olsen's claim that the author's decision to carry four children to term (in a time when abortion was a common alternative) may have had quite an impact on Olsen's own silencing as a writer. While we must not confuse Olsen's own identity with that of certain of her characters, there is an obvious connection between the two. Her interest in issues surrounding the female experience is a personal one in many ways, for she was herself a worker, a mother, a member of the community, and a participant in a social revolution. In fact, in *Silences*, Olsen cites African American playwright Ntosake Shange as confirmation of the difficulty of separating a woman's life experiences from her writing: "When women do begin to write ... we write autobiography. So autobiographically in fact that it's very hard to find any sense of any other reality" (242). Olsen, perhaps more so than Sanger, recognized the state of captivity in which most working-class women found their bodies; she then utilized her ability as a writer to give voice to certain experiences that have been dismissed in other working-class writings, namely pregnancy and childbirth.

Olsen's writing is crucial to study because she sees that in captivity of the body, as one may describe pregnancy, a painstaking but nevertheless necessary path toward creative rejuvenation is not only possible but probable. Mara Faulkner observes that there are "oppositions all of Olsen's work holds in balance: urgency and anger but never despair; hope, but never a serene or cynical acceptance of the intolerable conditions fragmenting the lives of the people with whom she identifies" (2). In *Silences*, Olsen condemns what she calls the "patriarchal injunction," or the assertion that in order to be taken seriously as a writer, a woman must avoid all subjects that mark her as a gendered being. Naturally, a reading of pregnancy would fall into such a category of subjects, yet Olsen successfully interests the reader in how mothers speak in her narratives, and maternity is lifted to the level of serious contemplation. She is not one, like Gold, to idealize this maternity; in fact, she refers to it as "the least understood, the most tormentingly complex experience to wrest to truth" (*Silences* 254). One of the main arguments in Olsen's book is that there is only one woman author of achievement for every twelve men, in the sense of being published and receiving recognition for their work. Her determination to write about the silenced is fueled by a desire to understand such a discrepancy, and she concludes that women have long lacked "the will, the measureless store of belief in oneself to be able to come to, cleave to, find the form for one's own life comprehensions" (27), largely due to societal expectations of gender. Olsen seems to argue along the same lines as critic Elaine Showalter in emphasizing that women have not seen their own individual experiences portrayed in literature and thus are often not as confidant in the value of their own observations.

Obviously, women *have* written and written powerfully, but Olsen notes, disturbingly, that most of the most influential women writers of the twentieth century have been unmarried and childless. Olsen does allow that "more women writers in our century, primarily in the last two decades, are assuming as their right fullness of work and family life" (31), and she includes a comprehensive footnote within her text naming these writers. Regardless of this acknowledgment, she adds that "not many have used the material open to them of motherhood as central source for their work" (32). Olsen includes in a footnote poet John Berryman's warning to women who write: "Woman, this is man's realm. If you insist on invading it, unsex yourself—and expect the road to be made difficult" (31). Olsen recognizes that a woman's writing of her own maternity both problematizes and somehow delegitimizes both her stature as a writer and the actual writings that come out of such experiences. On the front jacket of a recent version of *Silences* is Maxine Hong Kingston's declaration that Olsen's is "a valuable book, an angry book, a call to action"; Kingston, who writes of and values the maternal experience herself, is a nice companion voice for that of Olsen, as together they hope to disprove and dismiss any accusations of biological limitation. Moreover, Olsen argues that the angst that maternity inspires is balanced by the contributions that these experiences have had to her work; indeed, the publication of *Silences* has had an enormous and direct impact on women writers who would write after Olsen.[7] In fact, Tillie Olsen's name and *Silences* are as important to contemporary feminist studies as Virginia Woolf's, and her influential and much studied *A Room of One's Own*, have been to many generations of women, yet Olsen's name remains relatively obscure even to a well-read graduate student in English. While a graduate student might come across Olsen in a survey course and read a story from *Tell Me a Riddle*, Olsen's critical and creative work has yet to penetrate the mainstream canon in a significant way. She seems to be very much *the* feminist theorist for those contemplating pregnancy, childbirth, and motherhood and how these experiences penetrate aspects of intellectual and philosophical existence. As Fishkin points out in her introduction to Olsen's book,

> *Silences* has helped change what we read. It has given scholars and publishers the confidence to approach buried and forgotten texts with fresh eyes and new understanding, to appreciate journals and other private writings, and to read in women's artifacts (such as quilts) stories and plots invisible to previous generations (xvi).

The experiences of pregnancy and childbirth have indeed been dismissed in various texts as minor experiences connected to the experience of motherhood, even though in and of themselves they are experiences worthy of serious attention. Certainly the experiences of pregnancy and childbirth are often marginalized in working-class texts to what most consider the larger problem of poverty, but Olsen was determined to highlight pregnancy and childbirth in a little known masterpiece called *Yonnondio: From the Thirties.*

In *Tillie Olsen: A Feminist Spiritual Vision*, Elaine Orr observes that "dauntless courage and resilience is a hallmark of Olsen's characters, especially her women" (104). Moreover, in *Tillie Olsen: A Study of the Short Fiction*, Joanne Frye concludes, with regard to Olsen's work, that "we *do* find in these fictional pieces new understandings of human lives, especially of the lives of women" (13). Frye further writes of Olsen as an innovator in the construction of a "maternal narrative" which she describes as "both an unusual literary subject matter and a powerful narrative innovation" (24). Through Olsen's constructing such a narrative, Frye believes that Olsen becomes rhetorically effective in building a bond between narrator and audience so that the audience becomes responsive to the mother's concerns. Olsen therefore grants her narrator the "capacity to select, to describe, and to interpret based on a much richer and more empathetic knowledge than would be available to any other narrator" (Frye 31). Olsen's unfinished novel *Yonnondio: From the Thirties*, composed between 1932 and 1936 but unpublished until 1972, is unique to Olsen's body of work in that it not only seeks to investigate the experience of motherhood but also the condition of pregnancy, and Olsen's novel is indeed viscerally felt and a torturously evocative maternal narrative that includes pregnancy and childbirth as important aspects of the "maternal" narrative. Orr calls this novel "a story of limitations that miraculously yields a vision of hope" (67), though initially as one settles into the narrative it seems implausible to think that the story of the Holbrook family is anything but hopeless. As Michael Staub observes in "The Struggle for 'Selfness' Through Speech in Olsen's *Yonnondio: From the Thirties*," the novel is most definitely about Anna and her daughter Mazie, "and their efforts to speak and be heard in a hostile environment" (131), an environment that includes the volatile husband and father Jim Holbrook, a frustrated worker seeking substantial employment and respect in a harsh economic climate.[8]

While the reader does muddle through Jim Holbrook's own desperate and painful journey, Olsen insists that our concentration be on the women in the text. Olsen identifies what will become obvious within the first few pages: that the women working alongside the men, sharing the uncertainties that go along with living in and amongst the coal mines, are attempting to locate a more favorable place for their families within such an economy. Their highest hope is for "the kid[s] to be different, [to] get an edjication" (2), and, pointedly, Anna, relating to her husband the hopes that a friend has for her children, says that her friend "wants the girls to become nuns so they won't have to worry where the next meal's comin from, or have to have kids" (2). Jim responds, in character, to such hopes by wondering "what other earthly use can a woman have?" (2). Although Jim Holbrook can be counted on to suppress his wife's dreams of more authority over the direction of her own life by issuing an order to "quit your woman's blabbin'" (3), Staub argues that it will be through such "blabbin'" that the "women and girls of the working class will ... identify their own concerns at home or in the society at large, and will ... be able to change their lives for the better, [by creating] forums where their individual stories are heard, shared, and debated" (131).

Elaine Orr argues that beginning with *Yonnondio*, "we have in Tillie Olsen's work a shaping maternal consciousness, a political and spiritual voice arising from mothering realities" (52). Anna's character quickly becomes central to the narrative, and we experience her a great deal through her interaction with her daughter, Mazie. Anna's frustration is magnified when she looks at how her daughter "all of her six and a half years was like a woman sometimes" (3); in fact, Mazie is often pictured as the caretaker of her younger brother, "warming the infant to her body," changing diapers, quieting his cries, virtually functioning as the mother of the baby when Anna's attentions must be elsewhere. Traditional gender roles, Orr argues, "are limiting and unjust, but at the same time clearly reflect Anna's (and Mazie's) work as essential to the family's well-being" (53). Most problematic is how Jim assumes ownership of Anna's body and how she therefore becomes "the victim of Jim's ravenous hunger...not for food or sex, but for his manhood, [and] for the human dignity that is being taken from him" (Faulkner 41). Faulkner further underscores her assertion by arguing that Anna's numerous pregnancies are "the inevitable result of Jim's attitude toward her" (41), implying that he can only feel a part of production in reproduction. Olsen, in Mara Faulkner's opinion, paints pregnancy as a parasitic experience, arguing that "mothers living in poverty are doubly starved, bearing their children's deprivations as well as their own" (41). Although such points are well taken, Anna's experiences of pregnancy, childbirth, and the continuation of "giving birth to" her children through nursing are more than merely parasitic—they take her both to the lowest depths and to the greatest heights.

Mickey Pearlman and Abby H. P. Werlock argue that "Anna's fertility is contrasted with the barrenness of her family's future, and the reader is reminded that repeated and often unwanted pregnancies degrade women, particularly poor, undernourished women, and that the actuality of pregnancy contrasts markedly with its usual (and usually male-created) Madonna manifestations in literature and art" (43). Certainly Anna's body does seem ravaged by her successive pregnancies, but she is also granted some release from the grind of her daily life when she is pregnant with Bess as well as in the aftermath of her miscarriage. Olsen paints a portrait of a woman who is actively trying to make her family more secure, but she is not idealistically portrayed as prototypical Madonna; instead, she is always portrayed realistically, and, some might think, negatively—at times losing patience and her temper with her brood. Something changes when Anna becomes pregnant with Bess, and we are given an indication that this pregnancy has allowed her some temporary psychological escape from the grind of her daily life. Olsen writes, "Anna was pregnant again—caught in the drowse of it, drugged by the warmth, she let things be" (56). Naturally, Anna's inactivity only heightens Jim's frustrations, and he resents the "dirty clothes gathered into a waiting pile, [the] bacon drippings coiled greasy in the bottom of the pans, [the] bread that went unmade, and the smell of drying diapers layered over the room" (56). While everyone around her is wanting in one way or another, either for attention or food, Jim envies Anna's ability to use her pregnancy as a way to remove herself mentally from the harshness of daily existence. She becomes, in his eyes, vampiric, growing "monstrous fat as if she were feeding on them" (56).

The reader recognizes this reprieve as all too brief, noting how Anna's body is in a constant state of either preparing for childbirth or recovering from childbirth; in fact, there is not a time in the novel when Anna is neither pregnant nor nursing, and the physical toil that it takes on her body is striking. When the family moves to the city so that Jim can find work at a packing house, Anna loses the resilience that she had while they were living in the country. Olsen writes that "into her great physical pain and weariness Anna stumbled and lost herself" (81), after which she retreats even further from her family. With regard to the housework and childcare, "she could not really care" except for sometimes, "nursing the baby, chafing the little hands to warm them" (81). Anna's physical connection with Bess, the physical pull of her sucking at her breast, brings both her only comfort and her eventual resignation. In one particularly striking image, Mazie relates how Anna's life has literally been sucked out of her by her own child: "In the dirty light of dusk her mother sat motionless, her eyes large and feverish, the baby at her breast asleep. The lifeless hair hung in two black braids, framing her like a coffin, and above the spiral of fire foamed, reflected from the open damper" (103). This image shows how Anna is ominously surrounded by the signifiers of a constrained maternity; and, away from the country and in the city, living near the filthy packing houses, with its violent "smells of vomit" (79), she has lost hold of herself. Shortly thereafter, she suffers a miscarriage; in trying to nurse her child, she has depleted the nutritional stores necessary to keep the baby growing inside of her. It is in response to Jim's demand for intercourse that the bleeding begins, and she miscarries the baby she had no idea was growing inside of her. Oddly, though, it is also at this moment in the novel that we note a significant turn—help comes in the form of a housekeeper and caretaker for the children—and it is also at this point that Jim's apparent roughness begins to show vulnerabilities. Because of Anna's inability to care for the family, he must fill her role, and in doing so, he learns (albeit minimally) to appreciate his wife's strength.

Just as Olsen's narrative is intentionally illustrative, especially with regard to the violent smells and sounds the Holbrook family is forced to endure, her style is engagingly poetic. Just as Rebecca Harding Davis creates the workplace in her "Life in the Iron Mills" to be a living, breathing force, Olsen paints an ominous and life-like portrait of the mines that consume both the men who work them and the families who must live near them. In the opening pages of her novel, Olsen beautifully eulogizes the most recent victim of the mines, Andy Kvaternick, by speaking of the "dreams—vague dreams, of freedom and light and cheering throngs and happiness" (4) that he formerly held. Olsen chooses metaphors of pregnancy to describe how the earth takes these men's lives, growing "monstrous and swollen with these old tired dreams, swell and break, and strong fists batter the fat bellies, and skeletons of starved children batter them, and perhaps you will be slugged by a thug hired by the fat bellies" (8). Olsen also chooses the language of pregnancy to describe how Mazie's fear grows in response to her father's violent rages as "she clutch[es] the baby closer to her, tight, tight, to hold the swollen thing inside" (10). Moreover, as Mazie watches her father bathe, "nude, splashing water on his big chunky body," his figure is suggestive of a pregnant form, though pregnant with hostility, fear, and loathing for his own life. Mazie holds the infant as she watches her father, feeling "some alien sweetness mixed with [fear]" (10), and with this image Olsen illustrates the ways that pregnancy and fear can be devastatingly intertwined.

Later in the text, when Anna is pregnant again, Mazie is forced to confront the largeness of Anna's belly, and, once again, Olsen conflates pregnancy with violent imagery. Seeking solace during her mother's early labor, Mazie turns "to the sky for oblivion" (61), but the same sky that is usually a source of solace for her becomes only "swollen bellies, black and corpse gray" (61). Mazie, therefore, must come face to face with the "blood and pain of birth" (61). Not only must Mazie share the same space with her mother during the childbirth, but she is actively enlisted as a participant in the endeavor. Olsen paints a formidable scene in which "the black gates of [Anna's] eyes opened on something too far to see to" (61), suggesting the wariness she feels in enduring another childbirth. Mazie's fear is viscerally felt, as she repetitively speaks the words, "Momma," "Yes, Momma," "I'm sick, Momma" in response to her mother's instructions while Anna endures the birth with "her face set," Olsen writes, "like a mask, purified, austere" (62). After the birth Mazie runs out into the yard, looking up at the sky but seeing only "a strange face, the sky grieved above her, gone suddenly strange like her mother's" (63). Through Mazie's interpretations of the scene, Anna is portrayed here as nothing less than a courageous warrior determined to prevail, and as readers, we "feel both a tie with the emerging life and a repulsion toward the harsher realities" (Orr 59).

Tillie Olsen has been quoted as saying that "you can't talk about loss without talking about gain" (Pearlman interview, 1987). Elaine Orr characterizes such hopefulness as Olsen's determination to show the "love and oppression that characterize mothering in our culture [which] offers complex insights to feminist readers trying to chart the avenues of women's search for meaning" (108). Though it seems almost inconceivable from reading most of the novel, Anna does finally reclaim some strength, and it is through experiencing herself as a child-bearing body that she is able to get "back in command, reclaimed, wholly given over" (154). She makes a pilgrimage of sorts with all of her children, "to a stretch along the river bluff, yellow and green and white with flowers and grass and dandelion glory" (142), during which trip Mazie notices how "that look was on her mother's face again, her eyes so shining and remote" (145). Olsen writes further that "the mother look was back on her face, the mother alertness, attunement" (147). At the "end" of Olsen's unfinished novel, Anna is completely reinvigorated, canning jars of fruit in order to make money, feeling "the human drive work in her; human ecstasy of achievement, satisfaction deep and fundamental as sex: *I achieve, I use my powers; I! I!*" (191). She has indeed been able to find freedom within a confined space, and she appreciates that her body, once held captive by successive pregnancies, is actually a vessel of empowerment. Anna has, in a sense, given birth to herself anew when she revives to return to the helm of her family. There is an amazing sense of hope in Anna's voice in the end, when the reader hears how "the fetid fevered air rings with Anna's, Mazie's, Ben's laughter; [and] Bess's toothless, triumphant crow" (191). Olsen seems to conclude that the "heat misery, [and] rash misery" has been "transcended" (191); and, finally, Anna tells Jim that "the air's changin" (191). Surely Olsen's intent is to promote a transcendent message, offering the reader deep connection and hope; nevertheless, she does not do this by presenting simple or idealistic images of pregnancy, childbirth, and motherhood. Instead, she acknowledges these experiences to be some of the most difficult, constraining, and often debilitating in a woman's life

Meridel Le Sueur, a social activist and working-class writer much like Olsen, has been criticized by many who consider her presentation of maternal issues such as pregnancy idealistically drawn. Indeed, Meridel Le Sueur's "Annunciation" is widely believed to be based on Le Sueur's own pregnancy during the Depression, and it reads more like later contemporary pregnancy memoirs that will be discussed in the last chapter. As a result, it marks a turn in women's writing of pregnancy in its poetic exploration of the positive possibilities inherent in this experience. Of all her contemporaries, Le Sueur arguably takes the most extreme approach to the body in categorizing pregnancy and childbirth as transcendent experiences. Images of pregnancy in works such as Meridel Le Sueur's "Annunciation" present the condition as a life-affirming one, a time of self-discovery when the narrator's writing is at its sharpest, her mind acutely observing and reporting on her surroundings. Le Sueur's pregnant narrator believes that because of her condition she is in a higher state of understanding, and her autonomy is at its pinnacle; her pregnant state has allowed her to transcend the squalor of her Depression-era environment, thus leading her towards moments when she feels she is truly alive and not "cold and hard and closed to the world" ("Annunciation" 1826). Anticipating the pregnancy memoirs of Louise Erdrich and Carole Maso, Le Sueur describes her narrator's pregnant condition as a sort of a temporary reprieve from the mental and physical impoverishment of the Great Depression.

From early on in the story, the narrator of the story expresses a need to capture this transformative experience in writing, and Le Sueur expresses through her narrator the intellectual relevance of examining pregnancy. Just as the narrator laments the dearth of such examinations in previous works of literature, noting that she's "never heard anything about how a woman feels who is going to have a child..." ("Annunciation" 1827), she is compelled to rewrite this experience as her own, dismissing what various manuals and textbooks say, and even the remarks of her contemporaries on her condition. In fact, Le Sueur's narrator faces many obstacles in viewing her experience in a positive fashion. After all, she indicates that she is an actress and writer who is having much difficulty finding work in a dreadful economic environment. Not only is no one around her celebrating the fact that she is going to give birth, she is openly urged by her partner and various others to "get rid of it" ("Annunciation" 1824). In light of all of the negative responses that she receives, the sense of tranquility that radiates through her words is remarkable; even as she speaks of walking the streets of San Francisco utterly famished, she is able to rejoice in the inspiration that this child has encouraged within her: "I had a feeling then that something was happening to me of some kind of loveliness I would want to preserve in some way" ("Annunciation" 1824). She indicates from the outset of the story that her pregnancy has prompted a sort of rejuvenating creative process that will guide her through the difficulties of carrying a child unwanted by the larger community, and this inspiration manifests itself in the form of writing. The child itself also becomes a creative work that is waiting to spring forth, to become "a warrior...fierce for change" ("Annunciation" 1825). As the title of the story intimates, she establishes the experience as a sacred event, one that has allowed her to express "something I want to say, something I want to make clear for myself and others" ("Annunciation" 1822). Le Sueur spends a great deal of time early on in the narrative describing the narrator's surroundings and how she reacts to these surroundings in her pregnant state. The narrator is quite clearly living a hand-to-mouth existence, rooming at a boarding-house that is rat-infested and home to those who are "waiting for death" ("Annunciation" 1823), but instead of finding herself appalled by these lamentable surroundings, she experiences the house as a place that "has become a kind of alive place to me" ("Annunciation" 1823). Furthermore, she communes with the natural habitat around the house, likening herself to one of the pears hanging from the pear tree, transposing her own body with that of the tree, which is indeed alive and thriving amidst decay and ruin. She believes that, like the tree, "such a bloom is upon me at this moment" ("Annunciation" 1825) that her condition overpowers her current state of despair.

Like Anna in Olsen's *Yonnondio*, Le Sueur's narrator is captivated by her pregnancy, though obviously in a more dramatic fashion than Anna ever allows herself to experience. Both characters are attempting to locate a place outside of their negative surroundings by using their bodies as guides to displacement of mind, and they (consciously or unconsciously) use pregnancy as a means by which they visualize themselves into a more serene space. Le Sueur's narrator recalls how she has been able to overcome the agonies of rotten food and miserable quarters by feeling the thickness of her pregnant form. Even amidst the despair, the narrator comments that "for some reason I remember that I would sing to myself and often became happy as if mesmerized there in the foul room. It must have been because of this child" ("Annunciation" 1824). As readers, we are privy only to her "writings about" the writing of her experience and can imagine only what she puts down on paper. These elusive writings are referred to as thoughts scribbled down on "little slips of paper"; implicit in this is a desperation to document the ever-changing nature of her mind and body, and her scribbling represents her "trying to preserve this time for myself so that afterwards when everything is the same again I can remember what all must have" ("Annunciation" 1827). She senses that any audience will have a difficult time comprehending her thoughts: "It is hard to write it down so that it will mean anything" ("Annunciation" 1827). Like Mary Rowlandson, who must have felt a similar difficulty in describing her experiences in captivity, Le Sueur's narrator wants to record the experience so that it *does* mean something, so that she can guarantee such a release from other confinements in the future. In fact, Le Sueur's narrator admits to never feeling as alive as she does during pregnancy: "My hips are full and tight in back as if bracing themselves. I look like a pale and shining pomegranate, hard and tight, and my skin shines like crystal with the veins showing beneath blue and distended" ("Annunciation" 1827). The narrator's experience becomes one far beyond a short-sighted lament over economic hardship when she writes, preferring to think of the condition as a state of privilege: "I would like to read these things many years from now, when I am barren and no longer trembling like this…" (1827). Le Sueur's "pregnancy journal," as it might be called, becomes a conduit through which power and enlightenment might pass from one woman to the next, reflecting how women might use their bodies to defy societal impositions made on the pregnant and childbearing body.

Lest Le Sueur be remembered as hopelessly idealistic with regard to the condition of pregnancy, one need only turn to "Women on the Breadlines," her most famous short story, to reflect on what pregnancy and childbirth might cost a woman. In describing one of the women who come to the unemployment office, a Mrs. Gray, Le Sueur sadly observes that "her body is a great puckered scar" (1821). The account in this story is similar to the numerous ones collected in Sanger's *Women in Bondage*, another testament to how desperate economic conditions compromise both the bodies and minds of working-class women. I would argue, however, that Le Sueur's "Annunciation" is not an attempt at white-washing the gritty realities of working-class life. After all, as Linda Ray Pratt argues, Le Sueur was very much involved in the daily realities of pushing "the cause" through to manifestation.[9] Hers is a unique attempt to reclaim the experience of pregnancy as one that is both transformative and valid by counteracting the notion that women's bodies and biological destiny only compromise their ability to voice both political and social messages. Although Pratt calls "Annunciation" the "least directly political" (262) of Le Sueur's works, it is actually her most political in terms of rewriting the language of the female body and, in turn, arguing for an inclusion of such within working-class literature. The narrator's revision of societal control of self is appealing in its radical message about a woman's right to read her pregnant condition as she sees fit. Le Sueur has been labeled as one who encourages the perpetuation of motherhood at a time when social revolution is more important than reproduction, but by writing of pregnancy in this fashion, she in fact revolutionizes how later writers will characterize the experience—as is evidenced in the work of Louise Erdrich and Carole Maso and the proliferation of pregnancy journals that have followed into the twenty-first century. Le Sueur's piece rejects the notion that the only way out of misogynistic and/or economic captivity is to denounce pregnancy as a compromising condition; in turn, she actively promotes an understanding of women's bodies as repositories of worldly reflection and insight.

As Pratt points out, Le Sueur's feminist readership has noticed in her work a dedication to the female experience in her portrayal "of lives seldom represented in literature, and in her treatment of male-female relations" which suggests "a picture of sexual oppression" (258). Pratt further observes how the revival of interest in Le Sueur's work "centered on her presentation of the lives of women and not primarily on her class analysis" (247). Certainly these two problems are broached in conjunction in her *The Girl*.[10] Paula Rabinowitz argues in "Maternity as History: Gender and the Transformation of the Genre in Meridel Le Sueur's *The Girl*" that Le Sueur takes the working-class genre in a different direction through highlighting the unexplored domain of women workers, so often disregarded in the literature of Michael Gold and other male working-class writers. This novel allows the reader to see both the male and female response to working-class life, but the focus is decidedly on the women who occupy the working-class sector of St. Paul. *The Girl* is told in first-person by an unnamed narrator who is new to St. Paul and therefore unschooled in the ways of city life, though she receives a speedy education in the ways of the world through Butch, with whom she falls in love, and, more importantly, through the circle of women who become her emotional mainstay. The narrator's naïveté and forgiving nature do not conceal the oftentimes brutal and difficult reality of daily existence for a woman in such a society. The narrator's companions are Clara, a prostitute who actually pays certain men if they make her feel something; Belle, a woman whose maternal nature seems a direct result of her imposed childlessness; and Amelia, another maternal figure and organizer for the Workers Alliance. Though these women's lives do not appear particularly provocative, their ultimate response to their impoverished world shows them rediscovering the extraordinary through a reenvisioning of the seemingly mundane experiences of pregnancy and childbirth. Through them, Le Sueur seeks to resurrect the female response to working-class existence in *The Girl* by exploring "a different terrain—marked by sexual brutality, childbirth, and domestic work" in "the kitchens and bedrooms of the working-class home" (Rabinowitz 539).

According to Rabinowitz, Gold had commandeered the direction of working-class literature "by linking the proletariat, and its literature, with masculinity" (538); and, in doing so, he dismissed the female experience altogether. Rabinowitz further argues that "Le Sueur gives voice to women's memories—usually echoing through a long wail of maternal pain and joy—within a narrative whose plot revises the classic proletarian novel" (542). If, as Rabinowitz asserts, Le Sueur is instrumental in reshaping the working-class novel, she accomplishes this through her fascination with the maternal body, especially with the ways that pregnancy and childbirth shape the female response. The novel begins in the German Village, an establishment owned and operated by Belle, her husband, and his brother where they subsist on the money made from selling bootleg liquor and Belle's famous "Booya," described by the narrator as "an elegant stew of chicken and veal and beef and every kind of vegetable" (*The Girl* 1). The first birth that we encounter in the German village comes with the delivery of Belle's cat Susybelle's litter. Le Sueur devotes considerable attention to the laboring of the cat, and Amelia reveals her philosophical nature when she remarks with regard to Susybelle, "She's a female like us...[,] don't know the father, she gives all she's got to make them come out whole healthy full of seed" (*The Girl* 6). This interest in a seemingly inconsequential birth is heightened when the narrator finds herself unexpectantly pregnant. The narrator's emerging sexuality plays a large role in the novel, and after she loses her virginity to Butch, she immediately goes to her circle of female friends for solace. Belle relates the circumstances of her first sexual experience and how it resulted in the first of many abortions that she would have to endure, matter of factly describing herself as lucky that she did not die after the back-alley nature of the first abortion. Amelia responds to the narrator's vulnerability by taking her to her breast, exclaiming, "O, the breasts of our women are deep with the great life of the people" (*The Girl* 54).

Amelia correctly predicts that this first experience will result in a pregnancy, and it is at this point in the novel that the narrator's observations about herself and the world become more philosophically reflective. Rabinowitz argues that "the girl's narrative voice changes after her pregnancy because, with Butch's death, she is always with women" and that the "memory of maternity is linked to history and class consciousness for women" (545). It is at this point that *The Girl* also clearly recalls "Annunciation" in terms of how the narrator relates to her maternal body: "I feel my own little belly and I know the body of all women and even my mama's hanging belly that never goes back in shape" (*The Girl* 54). While Butch's response to learning of the pregnancy is to recoil "like a snake had bit him" (*The Girl* 77), the narrator feels "a great root springing down and a great blossom springing up, like [her] hair sprang up out of [her] skull green" (*The Girl* 60). The contrast between the two is profound: while Butch rests all of his hopes for the future on the success of a planned bank robbery which constitutes the elusive dream of financial solvency, the narrator, though clearly desirous of a similar sense of economic independence, recognizes that inner fortitude can be equally compelling: "I had to smile. I had already robbed the bank. I had stolen the seed. I had it on deposit. It was cached. It was safe" (*The Girl* 85).

While the women within the text are painfully aware of the compromised circumstances in which they live, their responses do not reveal the same kind of desperation that we witness in the men. In fact, they seem to recognize an inherent weakness in the men whose lives they share, and this book is all the more compelling given that the men, who are often violent in their interactions with women, are not, in fact, maligned. Instead, the women seem to recognize their desperation and to empathize. In the end, all the men are dead, unable to forge ahead in the cause because of their inability to work together as a community, but the women are unified in their desire that their voices be heard. Le Sueur dismisses any competition among the women, choosing to present a unified front. Even as the girl experiences pregnancy in economically undesirable circumstances, this same pregnancy allows her to exit a state of oppression and to emerge re-born into a circle of caring and nurturing women. Le Sueur is careful to chart the narrator's pregnancy amidst the insurgence of the Worker's Alliance. In reflecting on the growing child within the narrator, Amelia speaks of how her own pregnancies invigorated her and how this invigoration of spirit is similar to that she finds in working with the Alliance. As momentum builds within the movement, our attention is turned to the numerous women who are carrying children, and this fact strengthens Amelia's resolve. In speaking with the pregnant women, Amelia exhorts, "you can't make bones without milk don't they know that?" (*The Girl* 123). Indeed, both the narrator's pregnant body and Clara's run-down frame—both in need of scarce milk—become symbols of the inequities of a system that fails to respond to the desperate physical and emotional needs of women. These two bodies finally and poignantly come together with the seemingly inevitable death of Clara and the birth of the narrator's child who becomes her namesake.

The childbirth scene is one of the most prolonged in women's literature; a full eight pages are devoted to the narrator's labor and eventual delivery, and these events are paralleled by the demonstrations for fresh milk, with Amelia at the helm of each. The childbirth scene is as much a demonstration of the collective strength of working-class women and their rejection of a peripheral position in the movement as is the actual demonstration out on the streets. Le Sueur paints a primal picture of regeneration, with the narrator observing "the bearing and suffering in us all, their seized bodies, bent bellies hanging, and the ferocity of their guarding" (*The Girl* 148). Finally, we understand in the collective "sound like AHHHHHHH of wonder and delight" (*The Girl* 148) as the women surrounding the narrator look into the face of the new Clara that they have realized a respite from the captivity of their respective environments. Not only is the movement at its strongest point yet, but the narrator also has a "full breast of milk" (*The Girl* 148) with which to nourish her baby. Critic Rabinowitz's analysis falls short of pure praise in her understanding of how Le Sueur's "evocation of femininity ... verges on essentialism, because it invokes women's biological capacity to bear children without interrogating the cultural platitudes surrounding motherhood" (545-6). I would argue, however, that Le Sueur bravely interrogates each and every cultural platitude within this novel and thus comes to the conclusion that it is through the maternal body, and not in denying its relevance, that women enter importantly into the working-class arena.

It is terribly unfortunate that some of the most powerful voices in pregnancy literature come from women who remain, at best, marginalized writers. While Margaret Sanger, Tillie Olsen, and Meridel Le Sueur have all had quite a substantial impact on both the women's movement and the literature that purports to follow their cause, their writings, before now, have not been carefully explored for the ways that they champion pregnancy and childbirth as captivating experiences in and of themselves. Le Sueur writes in her Afterwords to *The Girl* that it "should be the function of the so-called writer, to mirror back the beauty of the people, to urge and nourish their vital expression and their social vision" (149). Clearly, Sanger and Olsen carried a similar burden of responsibility for lifting the real-life experiences of women to the level of artistic expression. In explicitly recording the grim and exhilarating beauty of pregnancy and childbirth in the lives of working-class women, they give voice to women's experience as unique and valuable to the working-class and to society as a whole.

Notes

[1]Hélène Cixous's "The Laugh of the Medusa." *Feminisms*. New Jersey: Rutgers University Press, 1997. 347-362.
[2]Murphy notes that Gold (a well-known American political activist and writer and passionate voice for social change and human rights, especially in the 1920s) was the sole editor of the *New Masses* between 1928 and 1930, making proletarian literature the primary focus of the magazine.
[3]Although Sanger's name will forever be intertwined with positive strides she made in forwarding women's health, her arguing in favor of fam-

ily limitation as a tool by which working-class women would liberate themselves from unwanted pregnancies linked her unfavorably with the eugenics movement. This involvement taints her name still today. See <http://www.nyu.edu/projects/sanger/ms.writings.htm> for further information about Sanger's life and history of advocacy.

[4]The letters selected for publication came from hundreds of thousands of letters Sanger received in the 1920s, some of which survive at the Sophia Smith Collection and the Library of Congress. *MIB* was used as an effective public relations tool to illustrate the rationale for birth control.

[5]According to Kessler-Harris and Lauter, Michael Gold urged his fellow writers to use the workplace setting as "a major focus for art," but given that fewer than fifteen percent of women worked outside of the home, his "workplace" obviously did not include women's work in the home, and so "only small fractions of women's lives would find their way into art" (intro xi).

[6]Roberts's introduction is particularly effective at delineating Olsen's commitment to depicting the truth of working-class life.

[7]Although the response to *Silences* was overwhelmingly positive, there were those who felt the tone to be somewhat "whiny" and thus unproductive. Others also pointed out that she did not concentrate on enough writers of color who have been able to write despite unbelievable obstacles. In defense of Olsen, Shelly Fisher Fishkin points to all of the writers of color who name *Silences* as hugely influential in their own coming to writing.

[8]"Yonnondio" is an Iroquois term; used in Walt Whitman's poem of the same name, it means "lament for the aborigines." Elaine Orr notes in *Tillie Olsen and a Feminist Spiritual Vision* (1987) that Olsen's novel is "her attempt to give some voice to the largely vanished lives of American workers in the 1920s and 1930s, and thus, in part, an attempt to overcome the loss of history mourned by Whitman's poem" (41).

[9]Pratt describes in her article "The Case of Meridel Le Sueur" how Le Sueur "frequently reported from the scene of strikes and meetings, and throughout her life she participated in all kinds of Party activities in Minnesota, including writing leaflets, demonstrating, working in the Party bookstore and the Worker's Alliance, and holding office in the local and state Party organizations" (252).

[10]*The Girl* was not published in full-length book form until 1978, although portions of the novel were published in short story format from 1935 to 1947. Also of interest with regard to the publication of this book is in the Afterwords section where Le Sueur's writes that this "memorial to the great and heroic women of the Depression was really written by them"

(149). Le Sueur states that this novel is actually a compilation of stories that she heard and recorded after meeting with a group of women in a writer's group in the Workers Alliance.

CHAPTER 4

EMERGING FROM CAPTIVITY: HOW AFRICAN AMERICAN WOMEN WRITERS USE PREGNANCY AND CHILDBIRTH TO CONFRONT THE PAST AND CREATE THE FUTURE

> Whereas art misrepresents the bodies of white women, it generally ignores those of women of color. —Sue Ellen Case[1]

Audre Lorde writes in "The Master's Tools Will Never Dismantle the Master's House" that "it is a particular academic arrogance to assume any discussion of feminist theory in this time and in this place without examining our many differences, and without a significant input from poor women, black and third-world women, and lesbians" (22). Feminist philosopher Robin May Schott voices similar concerns in "Resurrecting Embodiment" when she contends that a dismissal of the struggles of black women in pregnancy and childbirth is not a progressive stance but, rather, "a symptom of the lack of racial consciousness of postmodern critics" (175). Whether or not Schott's assertion holds true, it *is* important to note the difficulty of reading all pregnancy narratives within the same contexts as white pregnancy narratives. Schott insists that we focus on the ways that "black women's health is affected by prevailing political conditions" (176). My hope is that in acknowledging a discrepancy between black and white bodies, we might begin to understand why the images of pregnancy and childbirth in African American women's writing are substantially bleaker than any of the images that we have studied thus far. For this reason and many others, this chapter will be perhaps the most important in studying literary images of pregnancy as illustrative of captivity. Like their working-class counterparts, African American women writers, as early as Harriet Jacobs, include a number of images of pregnancy and childbirth in their narratives and, again like working-class women writers, have ultimately carved out a niche in literature by carrying out a fearless interrogation of how pregnancy and childbirth further complicate the lives and consciousnesses of African American women.

This chapter analyzes how various African American women writers have boldly deviated from traditional images of pregnancy and how such gestures have resulted in an explosive confrontation with this experience. This chapter begins with a thorough discussion of Harriet Jacobs' nineteenth-century autobiographical novel *Incidents in the Life of a Slave Girl*. This work is an important example of how African American pregnancy narratives simultaneously demonstrate a racial and class positioning that does not simply result in a loss of subjectivity but also reclaims authoritative voice through a creative narration of individual experience. In just the last twenty-five years, Jacobs' text has been identified as one that significantly challenges the strict parameters of genre in depicting women thinking and writing powerfully about the body far earlier than many imagined. It is serving to open the door for later African American women writers Alice Walker, Toni Morrison and Sapphire. They, too, depict bodies steeped in captivity, bodies that are consistently inscribed with the values of a society that unfairly categorizes and demeans them. Jacobs' text is important here as a point of reference as to how the African American pregnancy narrative derives, at least in part, from such early slave narratives as hers. To be sure, within her slave narrative we encounter resiliency and courage, and we also confront, for better or for worse, how the female body figures prominently in such tales. A study of both the language of and the imagistic renderings of pregnancy and birthing in Alice Walker's *Meridian* and in Toni Morrison's *The Bluest Eye* are the primary focus of this chapter, although other relevant scenes from other novels by these authors, namely *The Color Purple* and *Beloved* are also considered. These two pivotal writers continue the nineteenth-century slave narrative through the articulation of the twentieth-century African American woman's experience of pregnancy and childbirth. This chapter explores how they created powerful narratives through unabashedly rejecting society's prescriptions for documentation of these conditions in favor of depicting candidly how such experiences are aggravated by the role that race plays in the equation.

Further, the risks that these writers have taken are continued today in the work of writers like Sapphire who has published a controversial text with the experience of pregnancy given considerable attention and concern. The author's chosen name belies her determination to refashion and rescript perceptions of the African-American woman's maternal body. Deborah Gray White writes that the construction of Sapphire is the new myth of black womanhood, replacing the older myths of the Jezebel (the hyper-sexualized slave) and the Mammy (the dependable, maternal slave). White finds this new mythic Sapphire growing out of "the numerous inaccurate interpretations of the black woman's history," but this new mythic woman does have potential even in her classification as a "domineering black woman who consumes men" (166). White describes Sapphire "as tough, efficient, and tireless as Mammy, but whereas Mammy operated within the boundaries prescribed for women, Sapphire is firmly anchored in a man's world" (166). White views all of these myths—Jezebel, Mammy, and Sapphire—as problematic in that they seek to subsume the entirety of the black female experience. Nevertheless, there is hope for Sapphire, the author of *Push*, that in reappropriating a myth of black womanhood she might individualize and thus redefine black women's history. Her pen name carries loaded potential, and she does not shy away from a confrontation with issues that are shockingly controversial. The works focused on in this chapter offer the female body in retreat; at other times, we see a celebration of the pregnant and birthing body as a means of creative expression outside the captive confines of literal and figurative slavery.[2]

Critic Nellie Y. McKay argues that "the efforts to reverse the negative images of black women in literature began as early as these women began to find an opportunity to write: with the slave narratives, fiction, poetry, and nonfiction prose of the nineteenth century" (153), and she then cites Harriet Jacobs' *Incidents in the Life of a Slave Girl*, published in 1861, as a "significant contribution" to African American women's writing because of its delineation of "the differences between psychological and physical freedom" (154).[3] Jacobs, a former slave living in the North at the time of *Incidents'* publication in 1861, published her text under the pseudonym Linda Brent. This date of publication, however, is misleading in that it suggests that Jacobs' text garnered significant attention earlier than it actually did. In fact, her text was virtually overlooked and not rediscovered until the early 1970s and not critically evaluated and praised until the early 1980s.[4] Since then, it seems, critics have turned repeatedly to Jacobs' text for insights into the experiences of women living in slavery, and Jacobs does indeed deliver a powerful and devastating portrayal of women in captivity.[5] Jean Fagan Yellin, regarded as the founding mother of Jacobs criticism, calls Jacobs' text a "peculiar example" (208) of the American genre of "slave narrative," though she argues that it is in the peculiarities that Jacobs creates an authentic form of writing—one that encapsulates the black woman's experience of emotional and corporeal captivity. There are numerous references in literature to those unfortunate female slaves who were sexually abused by their masters, but perhaps Jacobs' story is unique in its depiction of a protagonist who not only recognizes the power of her body but also uses it to minimize her master's control. In the narrative itself, Jacobs concentrates largely on the time between her mid-teen years and her late twenties, when she was attempting to evade the sexually predatory hands of James Norcom (whom she calls Dr. Flint in her text). She writes at a time in the nineteenth century, as White observes, "when the nation was preoccupied with keeping women in the home and protecting them, [when] only slave women were...unprotected by men or law" (162). It is best to begin with Harriet Jacobs' autobiography here because embedded within the text of this "slave narrative" is actually one of the first recorded African American pregnancy narratives.

Without a doubt, Dr. Flint's obsession with Jacobs is predatory, but it is also strikingly predictable. Flint hurls continued abuse on her not only because he is tormented by his desire for that which he views as disposable property but also because he is frustrated by Jacobs' continued evasion of his advances. Undermining further his understanding of the slave/master relationship, Jacobs willfully defies all stereotypes that Flint has of "slave woman" in her show of obvious intelligence and craft in evading his many attempts to control her. In fact, Jacobs' ensuing affair with a neighboring white landowner, Mr. Sands, becomes her only assurance that her master will not be able to control a body over which he ostensibly has categorical rights. Denied the right to marry the free black man with whom she falls in love, Jacobs chooses to protect herself against Dr. Flint by offering her body to Sands.[6] Pregnancy, in turn, becomes a way out of Dr. Flint's clutches and, importantly, her only chance to exert control effectively in what is otherwise a powerless position. With regard to slave women, White argues that "there was no reason for them to believe that even freedom could not be bought for the price of their bodies" (34). Sadly, though, Jacobs is finally unable to realize the power of her tactical maneuver because she must simultaneously confront the fact that her pregnancy defiles her in the eyes of her relatives. In one particularly moving excerpt, Jacobs relates how, after telling her grandmother of her pregnancy, she is temporarily thrown out of her house for what her grandmother sees as her sins against her entire family.

Nellie Y. McKay and Frances Smith Foster argue in the introduction to their critical edition of *Incidents* that in "using her body as the source of her literary authority, [Jacobs] demonstrated the nature of one of the most egregious evils of [slavery] by recording her account movingly and with the passion of a human being who understood slavery as a moral wrong perpetuated against one group of powerless people by another group made more powerful by dint of the ideology of racial inferiority and superiority" (x). While Jacobs' text was primarily written to aid in the abolitionist cause, its importance in forwarding an understanding of women's bodies, and maternal bodies in particular, cannot be underestimated. Indeed, Yellin argues that *Incidents* "challenges not only the institution of chattel slavery and its supporting ideology of white racism; it also challenges traditional patriarchal institutions and ideas" (209). Again, Jacobs' text stands out from other slave narratives in the simple fact that it is female-authored and candid with regard to "the issue of sexuality (and sexual abuse) between masters and female slaves" (Taves 211). Also critical is her recognition of how corporeal authority ultimately frees her from a lifetime of physical and emotional bondage. Later, after she has had her children and Dr. Flint still refuses to sell her and the children to Mr. Sands, she eludes his constant pursuits by hiding in the crawlspace of her grandmother's attic for seven years. Jacobs describes the space in the following manner: "The garret was only nine feet long and seven feet wide. The highest part was three feet high, sloped down abruptly to the loose board floor. There was no admission for either light or air" (92). Jacobs thus shows herself thus to be doubly captive—as a slave she is denied a position in society; as a captive in the cellar she is denied literal space and the company of her children. Interestingly, her literal captivity in the attic never serves to disempower her but rather fuels her determination to remain in control of her and her children's fates. Although her living conditions are dramatically uncomfortable, Jacobs finds solace in frequent glimpses of her children's faces through several small holes she bores in the wooden surface of her cell. In fact, these holes provide her with a one-way contact with the outside world, and she is able to overhear various conversations by people passing by. Jacobs spends ample time describing her confinement, relating battles with "hundreds of small red insects, fine as a needle's point, that pierced through my skin," and lamenting how "nothing but thin shingles protected [her] from the summer's sun" (93). Her endurance of all of these trials is made possible only by her confidence that she is doing the right thing for her children in remaining out of sight, and she is afforded a sense of power when she learns of Flint's repeated trips to the North to locate her, obviously to no avail.

What Jacobs begins in pregnancy—an emancipation of her body and mind—continues through those seven years in the crawlspace, becoming a commitment to justifying her decision to give birth to her children in the first place. Jacobs gives snapshots of the impact that her children have had on her life; of her first child she remarks, "the little vine was taking deep root in my existence, though its clinging fondness excited a mixture of love and pain" (53). As they grow older, she continuously refers to the high moral character of her children Benny and Ellen, and her pride in their development affirms her choices. Jacobs' first pregnancy is actually the initial step in her plan to recreate herself, not as slave but as a woman refusing a life of captivity, and while she is physically captive in the crawlspace, she continuously notes how her physical discomforts in her cell pale in comparison to a life without control over one's body and mind and, by extension, one's destiny. We see that Jacobs' choice to become pregnant and all of the successive choices were not "reckless" decisions, as she calls them, but rather calculated ones. She becomes the very essence of a heroic maternal figure in her dedication to the future freedom of her children, and she feels that this reward is sufficient to see her through the hardships: "I tried to be thankful for my little cell, dismal as it was, and even to love it, as part of the price I had paid for the redemption of my children" (98). As White observes in her study of the life of the female slave, "slave mothers adhered to mores that made motherhood almost sacred, mores rooted in the black woman's African past" (106). Similarly, Jacobs recognizes in motherhood something grand and significant; she views her situation and her choices as determining the later experiences of her children. Therefore, while she is a slave Jacobs recognizes what little control she has and puts it to use. When she is in hiding in the crawlspace, she carves out a space for her body, limited as it is, all her own. The ultimate victory is in her escape to the North where she finally is able to think and act freely and, ultimately, to write of and thus give voice to her captivity. Throughout the ordeal, Jacobs must use her body as a statement in the most extreme of fashions to protect the promise of self-autonomy; first, with her pregnant belly, she creates a physical and metaphorical wall in order to prevent Flint's penetration, and, secondly, she must contort her body in order to adjust to the miniscule proportions of her cell-like dwelling in her grandmother's attic. McKay views such autobiographical stories as Jacobs' as tales of empowerment, given that "ex-slave women took control of their narratives in much the same way as they took control of the circumstances that enabled them to survive and escape captivity" (155).

Certainly Jacobs perceives her body to be a text of sorts, and she manipulates it much the same way that she later manipulates the auto-biographical genre. She recognizes at a very early age how her body and particularly Flint's obsession with it might be manipulated in order to reposition herself within her society. Of course, it is far easier for those of us who have never endured such circumstances to view Jacobs' actions as miraculous feats that ultimately shape her into the writer who gives us an important text. The reality, however, must have been excruciating; forced at the age of fifteen into pregnancy in a desperate attempt to control her circumstances, Jacobs undoubtedly experienced unimaginable terrors that she probably did not feel the full repercussions of until much later. However, since Jacobs writes of her experiences as an adult and therefore with more mature perspective on the choices of her youth, she expresses with certainty that the choices she made she would make again. With Jacobs we have a miraculous beginning in African American women's literature—of candidly discussing the maternal body compromised as it is by race and class by those who seek to discipline and normalize it. Most importantly, she rejects the notion of pregnancy as another form of slavery. Jacobs insists on claiming her pregnancies as her own, both as experiences she has actually *created* with her mind and body, and as ones that ultimately define the direction of her life. Certainly later writers like Walker and Morrison had Jacobs' narrative or the stories of other women slaves in mind as they set out with greater freedom to write of pregnancy and childbirth as experiences which promise further self-understanding.

In Alice Walker's collection of essays entitled *In Search of Our Mother's Gardens,* she relates what she sees as a distinctive quality of literature written by black Americans:

> [B]lack writers seem always involved in a moral and/or physical struggle, the result of which is expected to be some kind of larger freedom. Perhaps this is because our literary tradition is based on the slave narratives, where escape for the body and freedom for the soul went together. (5)

While the struggles over racial identity and the much sought-after freedom associated with these struggles remains central in the analysis done on Walker's texts, the experiences of pregnancy and childbirth—which demand a similar investigation of freedoms of mind and body—have garnered no more than an afterthought in critical study of her work.[7] This seems a striking omission, for Walker boldly confronts pregnancy and childbirth. In several of her works, in fact, she suggests that these experiences are of important consequence, whether negatively or positively, in African American women's lives. Interestingly, Walker refers to Kate Chopin's *The Awakening* as a narrative written by a white author whose narrative style and purpose most closely resembles those of African American women writers, most notably Zora Neale Hurston's in *Their Eyes Were Watching God.* The commonality that Chopin and Hurston share, Walker argues, lies in their urgent pursuit of "freedom and experience [rather] than comfort and security" (6). Walker's only lament is the fact that she was not introduced to either author in her own studies. Her interest, similar to Tillie Olsen's championing of Rebecca Harding Davis, is in bringing such writers out of obscurity, a feat that she and others have been successful in doing over the past thirty years. Further, Walker writes stories because, as she says, "they are the kind of books [I] want to read" (7). Clearly Walker's is not merely a desire for a good story but also the sense of knowing that certain stories must be brought back into the pubic consciousness. This recovery is critical, and with this recovery we are learning new ways to approach texts, to read narratives of pregnancy, of childbirth more accurately. Walker realizes, in particular, that pregnancy narratives, which are scattered throughout her novels, must be told with painstaking candor in order to preserve their place of importance in the histories of the African American women of whom she writes. Some of these images of pregnancy are merely sketches, others are more developed, but all of them are critical in illustrating how the African American woman has often experienced pregnancy and child-birth as both the literal and figurative captivity of the black woman to a white, patriarchal society that has historically neither valued nor sought to understand her body.

In a speech made at Sarah Lawrence College entitled "One Child of One's Own: A Meaningful Digression Within the Work(s)" on Muriel Rukeyser Day, Walker stresses that writers like Rukeyser (a poet recognized for her commitment to treating the subjects of pregnancy, childbirth, and motherhood in her work) and Tillie Olsen have taught her to privilege "not merely the necessity of confirming one's self in a time of confronta-tion, but the confirmation of the child, the Life of One's Child, against the odds, always" (*In Search of Our Mother's Gardens* 361). Further, Walker admits,

> I, like many other women who work, especially as writers, was terrified of having children. I feared being fractured by the experience if not overwhelmed. I thought the quality of my writing would be considerably diminished by motherhood—that nothing that was good for my writing could come out of having children. (363)

Walker's decision to have a child, she says, came from a sense of per-sistent curiosity, and she equates her attempts to conceive a child with all of her other intellectual and social contributions:

My good days were spent teaching, writing a simple history book for use in black child-care centers in Jackson, recording women's autobiographies, making a quilt (African fabrics, Mississippi string pattern), completing my second book, a novel—and trying to become pregnant. (366)

In giving voice to the experience of pregnancy and childbirth, she chronicles her severe morning sickness in the first three months and the disturbing sense of displacement that the physical changes characteristic of the pregnant condition can incite. Still, Walker speaks of giving birth as a miraculous feat: "the one genuine miracle in life (which is, by the way, the basic belief of many 'primitive' religions). The 'miracle' of nonbeing, death, certainly pales, I would think, beside it" (367). Furthermore, Walker emphasizes how enduring were the many challenges presented by her maternal body; these forever changed her perceptions of herself and the world. She asserts that through such experiences she evolved into "a woman who had written books, conceived in her head, and who had also engendered at least one human being in her body," and she finally concludes that "her [daughter's] birth, and the difficulties it provided [them], joined [her] to a body of experience and a depth of commitment to [her] own life hard to comprehend otherwise" (369).

However, when we look specifically at Walker's fictional images of pregnancy and childbirth, all of the possibility for emotional and philosophical growth that Walker conveys so well in her own experiences is not immediately evident in the experiences of her heroines. In Walker's most famous novel, *The Color Purple*, written in 1984, Celie is ill-equipped to confront her pregnant body, and Celie is not the first or the last character in Walker's fiction to be taken by surprise by her own pregnancy and ensuing childbirth. Further, believing that she carries and gives birth to her father's children, Celie can voice such experiences only with detachment. For instance, Celie describes her first childbirth in a matter-of-fact fashion and, some might argue, with little emotion: "When I start to hurt and then my stomach start moving and then that little baby come out my pussy chewing on it fist you could have knock me over with a feather" (3). Actually, this seeming lack of emotion stems from the fact that she has never been afforded the luxury of emotion; she is acted upon with little regard for her own emotional well-being, and she quickly learns that reacting pragmatically, stoically, or without evident emotion keeps her from further hurt.

Though virtually Celie's entire life might be characterized as a captivity narrative in both economic and racial terms, her tale is similar to that of Harriet Jacobs, for in early life she is tormented and raped by a man she thinks is her father (who we later learn to be her stepfather) and later forced into actual captivity through a marriage to a man who has neither love nor respect for her and who prevents her from making contact with her sister, Nettie. Moreover, the children she bears by her stepfather are yanked from her at birth even as her "breasts [are] full of milk running down" (4). Celie's own wants and desires must lie dormant for most of the text. Just as Harriet Jacobs' pregnancies enable the path that she takes, so, too, does the maternal connection that Celie feels towards the two children who are given away to Corrine and Samuel define her path. Celie's journal-like retelling of her history, beginning crucially with the birth of her two children, becomes a way for her to navigate sanely through these experiences: the ultimate product is a brief but poignant narrative of maternity. Celie's pregnancies and births are not extensively written into the narrative precisely because she does not have the recognition of her body as anything other than a facilitator of work and a storehouse of pain. In order to survive, she has forged a sufficient distance between mind and body to save herself from complete devastation. We see evidence of this distance when Celie's recognition of her second pregnancy comes only after a conversation she has with a girl at church: "[she] say you git big if you bleed every month. I don't bleed no more" (6). Perhaps in the end when Celie manages to assert herself, she might be able to give voice to these experiences, but until then, Celie can use only euphemistic language to describe her condition—describing "The first time I got big" (10) how "I'm all the time sick and fat" (11)—and feelings of shame when her teacher realizes she is pregnant: "she see how tight my dress is" (11).

Celie's violated body and the compromised nature of her maternity most decidedly affect how she reacts to and experiences her body throughout her life and in her interactions with Mr.___ and with Shug. Her lesbian relationship with Shug signals a change in Celie's individual narration of experience by affirming her own wants and desires, ultimately rejecting the systems and beliefs of a community that has a history based in slavery and intimidation. Alice Walker is thus clearly interested in the damaged sense of corporeal authority African American women are likely to experience with regard to pregnancy and childbirth, and her publication of the earlier and lesser-known novel *Meridian* is further evidence of her determination to include this subject within her overarching examination of the role race plays in American women's life.

Walker's *Meridian* has long been considered one of the most important treatments of the fight for civil rights, particularly as experienced by women. The entire backdrop of the novel is the Movement, and we meet Meridian as she fights for rights for the guano plant workers in her small town, still engaged in her late middle age in protecting the rights of those with little or no voice. Meridian believes the revolution to be highly personal, and so she returns from the North to the South to remain "close to the people—to see them, to be with them, to understand them and herself" (31). At this point the novel flashes back to Meridian's development as a black girl amidst the burgeoning Movement and how her maternal body collided with her involvement, both initially inhibiting and ultimately enabling her to enjoy a sort of rebirth as a connective force. Like Celie, Meridian Hill is initially disconnected from her body, a natural result of having a mother who is too preoccupied to give Meridian an honest explanation of her developing sexuality. Therefore, Meridian allows her high school boyfriend Eddie to have his way with her even though "[s]he could not understand why she was doing something with such frequency that she did not enjoy" (61). Walker writes that Meridian's subsequent pregnancy "came as a total shock" (61) to her and not at all a pleasant one. This shock is the immediate result of significant chunks of misinformation she receives at the hands of women who seem willfully ignorant of any ability to control their reproductive destiny. For instance, from her mother-in-law Meridian learns that "it is not possible to become pregnant if love is made standing up" (63). Her mother, in turn, shies away from any discussion of sex, telling her "absolutely nothing, [expecting] her to *do* nothing" (60).

Meridian's mother, Mrs. Hill, who "was not a woman who should have had children" (49), is depicted as captive to a certain set of societal rules that prescribe that she marry and reproduce in order to feel "fulfilled." Gloria Wade-Gayles notes in "The Truths of Our Mothers' Lives: Mother-Daughter Relationships in Black Women's Fiction" how pregnancy becomes, for Mrs. Hill, "an uncomfortable prelude to a life of emptiness" (11). Pregnant with Meridian, Mrs. Hill not only feels distracted from her true self, but she also believes that her pregnancy entails an abandonment of any self-definition, that the possibility of living for herself has now been erased. In a chapter entitled "'Have you stolen anything,'" we read of Mrs. Hill's unfortunate decision to marry and have children, which results in her belief that her very existence has been stolen away from her. Walker writes how "in her first pregnancy" Mrs. Hill "became distracted from who she was. As divided in her mind as her body was divided, between what part was herself and what part was not" (50). She refuses the "domestic arts" in a willful attempt to separate herself from those she views as intellectually inferior, but, in doing so, she further alienates herself from a connection to anything or anyone. This distancing from her children and from her profession as a teacher, Walker writes, is "the beginning of her abstraction" (51).

Mrs. Hill's is not the only tragic portrait of pregnancy as woeful sentence. Meridian herself is unable to realize positively her pregnant condition in any concrete sense; neither is she able to see it as philosophically charged. Like her mother, she is not at the helm of her experience; pregnancy is imposed on them both—the unfortunate result of the society's prescriptions, in Mrs. Hill's case, or the result of Eddie's demands, in Meridian's case. In neither case is pregnancy something that these women individually choose; consequently, the uncontrollable swelling of their physical bodies only fragments them further from any part of themselves that they thought they knew.

Although these pregnancies might be described simplistically as just unwanted, Walker allows her characters to find meaning even from such disappointment. Instead of denying their fates, they eventually confront their feelings of emptiness and bondage as they simultaneously wrestle with the implications of their pregnancies. Meridian simply cannot *feel* anything when she is pregnant: "she did not want it. But even this was blurred. How could she not want something she was not even sure she was having? Yet she was having it, of course. She grew and grew and grew and grew, as pregnant women will. Her skin, always smooth as velvet, became blotchy, her features blunted; her face looked bloated, tight" (63). The physical changes that she undergoes force a self-confrontation, and such changes are met with contempt similar to that of Flannery O'Connor's Ruby Hill—a contempt that transfers onto the child when he is finally born.

Walker's female characters come to pregnancy from several different forms of victimization, so often these pregnancies are a prelude to doom or precursors of further entrapment. For instance, when Wile Chile becomes pregnant, Meridian sees it as her duty to get her off the streets, the same streets where Wile Chile, for better or worse, has survived for years on her instincts. In Wile Chile's efforts to escape from such "civilization," she heads back to the streets and is hit by a car: "running heavily across a street, her stomach the largest part of her, she was hit by a speeder and killed" (37). Wile Chile's narrative is quickly followed by the legendary story of "Fast Mary of the Tower," a woman who attended Saxon College (Meridian's fictional alma mater) in the twenties and had a baby in a tower on the campus. Fast Mary, fearful of the repercussions of her condition, concealed her pregnancy, muffled her own cries during childbirth, chopped the baby into pieces and fed these to the commode, was later found out by her parents and instructors and locked away in her room without a window, subsequently hanging herself three months later. So moved are the college women by the legend that they institute a ceremony called "Commemoration of Fast Mary of the Tower," and "any girl who had ever prayed for her period to come was welcome to the commemoration" (45). Perhaps less doomed is Meridian's fellow civil rights worker Nelda Henderson, although her narrative similarly reveals the seemingly inevitable negative effect early pregnancy can have on a woman's attempts to distinguish herself in society. Nelda's position in her family is that of caring for the multitude of children that her mother has, a woman who herself "lost her hair—bit by bit—during each pregnancy" (62); then she finds herself pregnant, a condition which significantly disrupts her involvement in the Movement.

As the above examples reveal, Walker continuously emphasizes the fecundity of her female characters, but the ease with which they procreate is not interpreted as a blessing but rather as a curse. Both Meridian and Nelda are confounded by their fecundity—pregnancy is often the result of a first sexual encounter, coming as they have barely moved out of adolescence and certainly before they are able to grow into their bodies and effectively understand such an experience philosophically. With such a pregnancy comes a certain dread of the maternal body and of maternity as self-captivity in all its negative connotations. Ultimately, Meridian does abandon her child, aborts another, and then has her tubes tied by a doctor who is more like a butcher than a legitimate practitioner.

Though many readers might interpret Walker's treatment of pregnancy and motherhood to be lacking in any overtones of empowerment, these experiences actually serve as necessary rites of passage for several of her female characters. In fact, Meridian finds that the only way to secure her voice is forcibly to deny further reproduction. She has seen how her pregnancies are the direct result of others imposing their wants and desires onto her. Meridian does, however, cultivate in her interactions with Wile Chile, Truman, Lynne, and several other characters the ability to nurture. Pregnancy and childbirth, Walker carefully argues, are not experiences that should merely "happen" to the body; rather, they should be personal explorations outside the control of others and willed by the individual. Although pregnancy and childbirth seem as if they are imposed upon these characters just as slavery was imposed on their ancestors, there is an active opposition to likening pregnancy to another sort of slavery in the ways that they actively try to reinscribe these experiences as ones that forward understanding of self.

Toni Morrison, like Alice Walker, has often emphasized in articles and interviews how all of the experiences surrounding motherhood have shaped and informed both her writing and her understanding of the world.[8] Critic Andrea O'Reilly agrees that pregnancy, childbirth, and motherhood are "central theme[s] in [her] fiction," and in her reflections on such issues, "both inside and outside her fiction, Morrison articulates a fully developed theory of African American mothering which is central to her larger political and philosophical stance on black womanhood in America" (83). Further, critic Paula Gallant Eckard argues that Morrison emphasizes in her writing the knowledge "that maternal experience centered in African American culture is not monolithic, but rather reflective of diverse and complex realities" (34). In "A Criticism of Our Own: Autonomy and Assimilation in Afro-American and Feminist Literary Theory," Elaine Showalter references the publication, in 1970, of Morrison's *The Bluest Eye* as the pivotal moment when "black feminist writers and critics began to make their voices heard within the literary community" (217).[9] Interestingly, Morrison claims that "with very few exceptions, the initial publication was...dismissed, trivialized, misread" (216), and that it was only with the 1993 Plume publication of the novel that both she and her characters won the audience they deserved.

Morrison's narrative style is imagistic and supple and perfectly constructed to foreground illustrations of the pregnant and birthing body. Although *The Bluest Eye* is narrated largely from the perspective of Claudia MacTeer, a woman remembering back to her childhood, the narrative structure fulfills its modernist intentions by keeping the reader looking for the "reliable" narrator while navigating through ever-shifting perspectives. The interior monologues that reveal the lives and histories of Pauline and Cholly Breedlove, parents of tragic protagonist Pecola Breedlove, are almost invasive in nature. We would rather keep these two at a distance because of the unimaginable horrors that they inflict on their child, but Morrison does not allow us that luxury. These characters are, in fact, fully realized and surprisingly sympathetic.

Morrison devotes ample time to Claudia's recollection of the formative events of one particular year in her life as she reflects on the placement of blame for Pecola's mental breakdown. The novel starts in an innocent enough fashion with Claudia, her sister Frieda, and Pecola all attempting to decipher their own budding sexuality. A fellow classmate, Maureen Peal, whose light skin, flawless appearance, and haughty attitude provoke both envy and hatred in the other girls, is *almost* successful in elaborating the secrets of menstruation to the girls. When Pecola questions the purpose of menstruation, Maureen answers that it is "for babies" because "babies need blood when they are inside you, and if you are having a baby, then you don't menstruate. But when you are not having a baby, then you don't have to save the blood, so it comes out" (70). Maureen's knowledge is precociously accurate at times; she even describes how the "like-line," as she calls the umbilical cord, delivers blood to the babies from the belly button. This particular discussion functions as a devastating portent that one of these girls will be denied the luxury of innocence with regard to her underdeveloped sexuality.

Morrison's heroine, Pecola Breedlove, is a young girl whose name is portentous given that she has little of the latter (love) and the former (breed) is violently forced upon her. Further, she is unfortunate enough to have a mother who comments on first seeing her daughter that while she was born with a "head full of pretty hair… [,] Lord she was ugly" (126), and she is nothing short of a tragic figure. First she is subjected to repeated taunts by classmates and members of her community, then she is raped by her father, and when Pecola's pregnancy becomes obvious, instead of becoming an object of sympathetic outreach, she is further marginalized and widely held in contempt by society. It is fairly obvious from early on that Morrison's intention is to force us to measure ourselves against her; after all, Claudia even admits in the end that looking at Pecola in her state of madness and decay, "all of her waste which we dumped on her[,] she absorbed" (205). Claudia and Frieda piece together Pecola's predicament from a word here, a phrase there, tidbits they overhear when they are out selling seeds in order to earn enough money to buy a new bicycle. The most disturbing element of the story, Claudia feels, is the lack of empathy for Pecola, the fact that "[the townspeople] were disgusted, amused, shocked, outraged, or even excited by the story." Instead of a compassionate "'poor little girl,' or, 'poor baby,' there was only head wagging where those words should have been" (190). Pecola's pregnancy, the tragic result of her father's rape, is not narrated through her own consciousness, so we are never allowed into Pecola's own thoughts but rather limited to the perspectives of those who collide with her, more often than not, in devastating ways.

One might argue that Morrison uses Pecola's unfortunate situation as just another way to show that pregnancy might spell doom, but, in fact, Morrison sees at the very least the hope for affirmation of existence in her ordeal. Claudia, in particular, sees in Pecola's pregnancy an opportunity to reclaim a sense of pride in her own dark skin color. She wants the baby in Pecola's womb to be validated by the community just as she wants her and Pecola's darkness to be as privileged as the Shirley Temple ideal:

I thought about the baby everybody wanted dead, and saw it very clearly. It was in a dark, wet place, its head covered with great O's of wool, the black face holding, like nickels, two clean black eyes, the flared nose, kissing-thick lips, and the living, breathing silk of black skin…. More strongly than my fondness for Pecola, I felt a need for someone to want the black baby to live—just to counteract the universal love of white baby dolls…. (190)

Unfortunately, Claudia's desire is not universal, and her hope that the greater community might affirm her own perspective is impossibly doomed. Since Pecola's pregnancy is the result of incest, the community feels an "overwhelming hatred for the unborn baby" (191), and its members are desperate to distance themselves from any relations with the Breedlove family.

Before we fully learn Pecola's fate, we read of the experiences of Pecola's mother, Pauline Breedlove, and of her desire to find a place in a society that continuously marginalizes her. Initially, Pauline's retelling of her own pregnancy experience shows her to have an increased sense of her own worth and value; in fact, she describes how she "felt good, and wasn't thinking on the carrying, just the baby itself" (124). For a poor woman with very little education, she is dedicated to nurturing the baby she is carrying, telling the reader how she "talk[s] to it whilst it be still in the womb" (124). Her sense of corporeal authority is challenged, however, in her internal narration of her labor and delivery of Pecola. Morrison gives the reader a glimpse into a medical establishment that dismisses Pauline's individual needs and cruelly trivializes her experience. For her part, Pauline attempts to retain control over her experience, painstakingly recreating the scene as she prepares to give birth, illustrating her own invisibility in the eyes of a doctor who "gloved his hand and put some kind of jelly in it and rammed it up between [her] legs" (124).

Pauline accurately surmises that the many interns who come through to examine her are using her less as a scientific training example and more as ammunition to fuel certain stereotypes about black women giving birth. She overhears the doctor say about her that "these here are women you don't have any trouble with. They deliver right away and with no pain. Just like horses" (125), and Pauline is careful to note that the young doctors do not look her in the eyes the way they do the white women. Just as Pauline tries to write her own pregnancy narrative, the medical establishment interrupts and tries to dictate her feelings. Therefore, to elicit their attention, Pauline determinedly exaggerates her pains with loud moans, telling the reader that the "pains wasn't as bad as I let on, but I had to let them people know having a baby was more than a bowel movement. I hurt just like them white women. Just 'cause I wasn't hopping and hollering before didn't mean I wasn't feeling pain. What'd they think? That just 'cause I knowed how to have a baby with no fuss that my behind wasn't pulling and aching like theirs" (125). She even shows great empathetic potential when she wonders why the doctors think that a mare doesn't experience pain in childbirth: just "'cause she can't say it, they think it ain't there" (125). While Pauline is no heroine, she does recognize her body as potentially powerful.

Ultimately, Pauline, like most of Morrison's characters, is too damaged to deflect the hostility she faces in favor of the kindness and love she might offer her child. Once she gives birth to Pecola, all of her potential for transformation leaves her when she is disappointed in the appearance of her child. She subsequently displaces her own disappointments onto the child who mirrors back to her own "inadequacies." As Andrea O'Reilly argues, it is Pauline Breedlove's disconnection from "her motherline"—what Morrison sees as a crucial, instructive maternal force that keeps the ancestral history intact—that "renders her incapable of nurturing and sustaining her daughter, Pecola" (87). Moreover, O'Reilly marks the moment of childbirth as the "central trope of the loss of maternal nurturance engendered by assimilation and the resulting displacement of the motherline" (87). Since Morrison allows the reader entry into Pauline's consciousness during her pregnancy and during childbirth, the reader realizes the potential she has for rewriting the white patriarchal script; it is a doubly devastating moment in the novel, then, when we realize that Pauline ultimately gives in to her own desire to assimilate and sacrifices her daughter to do so. That is, Pauline is unable to reject the interpellations of the white medical establishment, and when Pecola is born both black and female, "Pauline sees it as she herself was seen while in labor as undesirable, irrelevant, and unimportant" (O'Reilly 90).

In the end, Pauline is irretrievably captive to the white patriarchal system that tries to control her in childbirth, becoming a surrogate mother for the white child in her charge and painfully denying the needs of her own daughter. Pauline's neglect and complicity in Pecola's rape ensure that Pecola's fate is sealed. Like Claudia's and Frieda's seeds that never flower, Pecola's child dies before Spring, and she is forever scarred by the experience. Pecola is left a perpetual wanderer, appearing to her community as a soul who has lost all contact with reality. Although her pregnancy is tainted by her father's sins and is never allowed within the text to come to positive fruition, Claudia's retelling of Pecola's ordeal promises some sort of possibility for healing within the community.

With *Beloved*, Morrison revises her view of pregnancy as captivity, and attempts to study further, as Jean Wyatt argues, an "experience that Western cultural narratives usually leave out: childbirth and nursing from a mother's perspective" (211). Sethe is able, in a certain way, to explode the term captive, rewriting the script of her ancestors. In this sense, *Beloved* charts new territory in the African American pregnancy genre by allowing its protagonist to create a birthing space away from captivity, in a space that is free from restraint. We come to Sethe's late pregnancy and childbirth as she herself recounts her earlier days as a slave and her decision to kill her child to save her from slavery. The appearance of the dead child, who is reincarnated as Beloved, is the impetus behind Sethe's reconstruction of her own history, done in part to satisfy the curiosity of her daughter, Denver, and in part to provide some closure for both herself and for Beloved.

As we have with Harriet Jacobs' text, Morrison provides in fictional form a former slave's recollection of bondage and the dramatic lengths taken to break free from such captivity.[10] While the novel is generally somber and haunting in tone, Sethe's narrative of her pregnancy and childbirth is, without a doubt, the most hopeful of such narratives by either Walker or Morrison. In just a few pages, there is an explosive confrontation with the old forms, and Morrison manages successfully to exorcise the ghost of Pauline Breedlove in the control she grants Sethe with regard to her maternal body. The setting of this important scene is something of a primal space; Sethe endures labor both in the forest and on the riverbank, and, in doing so, she returns to a time and place in which women were once considered the overseers of such experiences. Critic Tess Cosslett views Sethe's banishment to the wilderness for delivery of her child as further proof of her oppression. I would argue that Morrison's framing of this scene, the re-telling of her experience in labor and delivery, is actually part of Sethe's own creative authorship of experience. Denver, the child she delivers, learns the story of her birth from her mother so well that she knows it by heart. She and her mother, Sethe, tell the story to Beloved, "how it really was, something only Sethe knew because she alone had the mind for it and the time afterward to shape it" (78).

Sethe is a literal captive—a runaway slave—at the time she is about to give birth, and she is also a much sought-after fugitive who is "all by herself ... [carrying] ... another baby she has to think about" (78). On the run, Sethe, in early labor, ultimately finds movement impossible because of her swollen feet. Just then, Amy, the runaway indentured servant, crosses her path. Amy's initial reaction is to bemoan her own bad luck in stumbling upon a creature who she thinks is not long for the world, but almost immediately she takes on a caregiver role. Amy's incessant chatter—mostly about how she is going to Boston to escape her owner, Mr. Buddy—is the unlikely music that plays along with the moans and few words that Sethe emits. Amy's chatter serves almost to disguise her thoughtful precision in alleviating Sethe's discomfort. In fact, Amy asks for very little from Sethe, so occupied does she become in fulfilling her role as the useful attendant. All she asks for is affirmation that she is, indeed, "good at sick things" (82). Sethe grants her this praise and more, continually referring to Amy simply as "good hands" and "strong hands." During the course of the night, Amy performs small miracles in quelling the swelling in Sethe's feet and in helping her toward an abandoned boat where Sethe can deliver the baby.

As Le Sueur does in *The Girl*, Morrison provides the reader with a candid and metaphorically rich account of Sethe's labor and delivery in what many would consider dangerously compromised circumstances. Ironically, the forest, the water, and the boat all turn out to be perfectly suitable environs in which to labor and deliver the baby. There is no talk of anesthetic, no sterile room with forceps; there is only the natural world serving as her birthing room: "As soon as Sethe got close to the river her own water broke loose to join it. The break, followed by the redundant announcement of labor, arched her back" (83). Crawling towards her delivery room, an abandoned, sinking boat on the Mississippi River,

> She had just enough time to brace her leaf-bag feet on the bench when another rip took her breath away. Panting under four summer stars, she threw her legs over the sides, because here come the head, as Amy informed her as though she did not know it—as though the rip was a breakup of walnut logs in the brace, or of lightning's jagged tear through a leather sky. (84)

In symbiotic rhythm, Sethe "reach[es] one arm back and grab[s] the rope" to support herself while Amy "fairly [claws] at the head" of the baby being delivered (84). Later, "Amy wrap[s] her skirt around [the baby] and the wet sticky women clamber ashore to see what, indeed, God had in mind" (84). The final moments are heightened with dramatic poignancy when Morrison reveals that the river water is actually overtaking the boat, "seeping through any hole it chose, spreading over Sethe's hips" (84). Nevertheless, the makeshift birthing room proves sufficient, and Denver finally makes her way into the world: "Sethe arched suddenly and the afterbirth shot out. Then the baby whimpered and Sethe looked. Twenty inches of cord hung from its belly and it trembled in the cool evening air" (84). Morrison recognizes how some might interpret the scene: "two throw-away people, two lawless outlaws—a slave and a barefoot white woman with unpinned hair—wrapping a ten-minute baby in the rags they wore" (84-5), but there are no ready interpreters, only her readers whom she implores to interpret the delivery of Denver, amidst the dankness of a sinking boat in the wilderness, as no less than a heroic feat, performed "appropriately and well" (84) by Sethe and the white indentured servant, Amy.

Not only does "the universality of female experience and the urgency of childbirth help to unite them" (Eckard 67), but this shared experience of birth serves to empower both Sethe and Amy sufficiently to allow them to see beyond the moment, towards a more secure and appealing reality for them both. Critic Paula Eckard notices how Amy actually acts in the traditional role of "doula," a woman who attends to the mother during her labor, supporting her through labor and immediately after childbirth. Eckard's observation is an important one because Morrison is without a doubt aware (given the depiction of Pauline Breedlove's compromised labor and delivery in her earlier work *The Bluest Eye*) of how the experiences of pregnancy and childbirth may be either enhanced through the integration of woman-centered care or detracted from through medical objectification. In granting Amy such a pivotal role within the narrative, she advocates for more attention to the woman's needs during such experiences. More importantly, Morrison is interested in the role that race plays in Sethe's ordeal and the way that her escape from slavery coincides with her delivery of Denver, a child that will never have to experience bondage as her mother has. In giving birth to Denver, Sethe, like Harriet Jacobs before her, *creates* experience, lifting the pregnancy and childbirth to the level of spiritual renewal. In doing so, she washes away some of her captive history as a slave.

According to Jean Wyatt in her article "Giving Body to the Word: The Maternal Symbolic in Toni Morrison's *Beloved*," Morrison constructs a new narrative form through an emphasis on Sethe's determination to define herself as maternal body; thus, the reader embarks on what Wyatt views as "a specifically female quest powered by the desire to get one's milk to one's baby—that features childbirth as high adventure" (212). To be sure, Sethe's delivery of Denver in Morrison's *Beloved* is a far cry from Pauline's delivery of Pecola, both literally and figuratively. While Pauline is ostensibly surrounded by modern medical accoutrements that might enable her to be at ease with her body and the ensuing childbirth, she is only further distanced from herself when she is treated like an animal by the doctors. Sethe, on the other hand, has none of the comforts of the traditional birthing room but actually comes through the experience with more validation for life and recognition of her own strength. Like Harriet Jacobs, Morrison's Sethe regards motherhood as initiating acts of bravery and selflessness, and both are committed to seeing their children free from oppressive slavery. Morrison, however, actually highlights the "reproductive feats of the maternal body" (Wyatt 213) to support the notion of Sethe (and Amy, through her involvement) as heroic figure. In championing what are often considered the quotidian experiences of pregnancy and childbirth, Morrison stands out not only as a writer who, as Haskel Frankel observes in a review of Morrison's early work, "is willing to report the ugliness of the world as ugly" but also as a writer "who can reveal the beauty and the hope beneath the surface" (47). And while critic Tess Cosslett is disturbed by the primitive nature of Sethe's birthing experience, she does note that Morrison successfully "creates opportunities for women's power, agency and skill in the act of giving birth" (46).

Whereas Jacobs evades most discussion of the actual realities of pregnancy and childbirth certain to offend her nineteenth-century readers, the contemporary work of African American writer Sapphire holds back little in her depiction of the pregnant and birthing body. In doing so, she is sure to offend some late twentieth-century readers in her graphic use of language and treatment of the subject. Sapphire's *Push* goes one step further than do Walker and Morrison in writing of African American pregnant and birthing bodies by not only confronting incestuous relations between a father and daughter but also in allowing the children born of this incestuous union to come to life as characters in the novel. We might see, as critic Brenda Daly suggests, that such depictions are paving the way for new and innovative voices within African American literature.

Sapphire's heroine Precious Jones, reminiscent in nature and naivety to Walker's Celie, is an illiterate girl who is raped repeatedly by her crack-addicted father and gives birth to two of her father's children because she believes that abortion is morally wrong. With regard to *Push*, "the novel's title refers not only to the physical act of giving birth, but also to the daughter/mother's act of giving birth to herself through language" (Daly 107). In the beginning, physically and sexually abused by both of her parents, Precious wonders, "why can't I see myself, feel when I end and begin," but still literally *pushes* to conquer her illiteracy in order to care for her children. A viscerally painful read, Sapphire's novel presents initially Precious' lack of awareness with regard to her situation, a horrific one of sexual and physical abuse that becomes routine (and thus all the more horrifying) that Precious must endure. The end result of the abuse at the hands of her father is, of course, her first pregnancy at the age of twelve, a pregnancy that is denied by Precious' mother until the actual labor pains hit. When Precious feels these first pains, her mother must confront the tangible evidence of the incestuous union, and her explosive anger is misdirected towards her daughter. It is difficult for the reader to see Precious' mother as anything less than evil incarnate; here is a woman who sexually molests her own daughter, watches passively while her husband sexually abuses their child, and then violently beats Precious when her husband leaves her after the first baby is born. Even as Precious experiences the first pains of labor she must endure unremitting and direct blows by her own mother. The child, a baby girl, is born with Down's Syndrome; as Precious describes her, her face is "smashed flat like pancake, eyes is all slanted up like Koreans, tongue goin' in'n out like some kinda snake" (17).

It is through Precious' first experience of childbirth and in her subsequent pregnancy, though, that Precious comes to a clearer understanding of the path that she must take to escape her unbearable situation. This awakening of sorts actually comes during the experience of childbirth. The reader marks the moment of Precious' recognition of the ill-treatment that she has received at the hands of her parents first when she is treated by the EMS worker with kindness and sensitivity and then later when she is similarly treated by the nurse in delivery: "I feel warm kindness from her I never feel from Mama and I start to cry" (18). Precious' attempts at literacy gain momentum within the alternative school, are largely due to the efforts of her teacher Ms. Rain, who champions and encourages Precious' attempts to better herself emotionally and educationally. Precious strides toward literacy coincide with her ability to read her living situation as horrific and intolerable. Whereas before she denies her pregnancy even to herself, she begins to view the second child growing inside of her as metaphorical of the growth of her mind: "Not that I didn't know it before but now it's like part of me; more than something stuck in me, growing in me, making me bigger" (62). She realizes, with the aid of her classmates, that she bears a responsibility to this child she is carrying, to get proper prenatal care, to speak to her baby while he is still in the womb: "Listen baby, Muver love you. Muver not dumb. Listen baby: ABCDEFGHIJKLMN-OPQRSTUVWXYZ" (66). Precious' second pregnancy, which comes at a time when she has made strides in her own literacy, is starkly contrasted with her remembrances of pregnancy at the age of twelve, when she had little idea what was occurring within her body:

I mean I knew I was pregnant, knew how I got pregnant. I been knowing a man put his dick in you, gush white stuff in your booty you could get pregnant. I'm twelve now, I been knowing about that since I was five or six, maybe I always known about pussy and dick. I can't remember not knowing. No, I can't remember a time I did not know. But thas all I knowed. I didn't know how long it take, what's happening inside, nothing, I didn't know nothing. (11-12)

After the delivery of Precious' son Abdul when she is sixteen, she does not return home to live with her mother; instead, she opts to reside in a halfway house where she is able to continue taking classes and continue improving her writing. So the literal and figurative movement away from the space where she has been long violated is pronounced. This distance, coupled with the support of Ms. Rain, furthers Precious' growth and maturation. Ms. Rain recognizes how her students, women who have been cast aside and expectations dismissed in their regard, through the act of writing can rewrite their own scripts and become inspired and empowered. Sapphire does not relent in her narrative, and later we learn that Precious has been infected by her father with HIV. Her children are spared, though, and like Harriet Jacobs before her, the realization that she will be able to direct positively the futures of her children is enough to keep her going. Sapphire's novel, while devastating in its portrayal of ignorance and abuse, ends with an uplifting vision of Precious, Madonna-like, holding Abdul in her arms, hopeful that his future will be brighter than her own:

The sun is coming through the window splashing down on him, on the pages of his book. It's called The Black BC's. I love to hold him in my lap, open up the world to him. When the sun shine on him like this, he is an angel child. Brown sunshine. And my heart fill. Hurt. One year? Five? Ten years? Maybe more if I take care of myself. Maybe a cure. Who knows, who is working on shit like that? Look his nose is so shiny, his eyes shiny. He my shiny brown boy. In his beauty I see my own. (140)

Like the writers who come before her, Sapphire rejects old forms in favor of creating an original lens so that we might witness, perhaps with more sensitivity, the ways that pregnancy and childbirth continue to be experiences that African American women struggle to define as their own, after so many years of having them defined by others. Certainly issues like incest and rape are difficult ones to treat, but in doing so, and in her use of violent and graphic language, these experiences, like the brutal experiences of female slaves, become means by which these women writers can begin to control the direction of their own narratives. Such brave stories are where the pregnancy genre is headed, as we will see in the memoirs discussed in the next chapter.

Alice Walker's *Meridian* and *The Color Purple* and Toni Morrison's *The Bluest Eye* and *Beloved*, like Chopin's *The Awakening* before them, have provided for authors like Sapphire a sort of blueprint on which to build freely more unique and rich illustrations of African American experiences of pregnancy and childbirth. Both novels show their main characters understanding birth to be a sort of major revising of script and recovery of authorship. Working fearlessly through feelings of shame, humiliation, and anger, these writers realize African American pregnant and birthing bodies as complicated and creative vessels all their own and not merely bodies on which others have laid claim. According to Naomi Wolf, "what is most distressing is not the prospect of labor and delivery honestly told, but rather the psychic cost to mothers-to-be of literature that is determined to focus on happy talk and sentimentality" (4). For many readers, Jacobs, Walker, Morrison, and Sapphire have successfully transformed so-called "negative" images of pregnancy into ones that hold the greatest potential for empowerment, even if such empowerment is not realized by all the characters involved.

Notes

[1]From Case's *Feminism and Theater*, p. 98

[2]Though my focus in this chapter is African American women's fiction, drama has also been bold in its confrontation of the problems that pregnancy presents. Ntosake Shange's *Spell #7* and Adrienne Kennedy's *A Movie Star Has to Star in Black and White* are perhaps some of the most important works to consider in that they attempt to show that the so-called "negative" images of pregnancy are the ones that, ironically, hold the greatest potential for empowerment. Through their elaboration of a woman's acceptance of the dangers of loss of subjectivity inherent in pregnancy, we can begin to explore possible ways of reclaiming that subjectivity. Neither Shange's nor Kennedy's characters have been allowed the freedom to express their own needs and desires. Not only are they abused by their society, but also their voices are silenced. In her analysis of the pregnant female in Kennedy's world, Claudia Barnett finds only

failed pregnancies—"pregnancies that end in miscarriage and madness" (141). Kennedy's dramas "present pregnancy and motherhood not as traditional symbols of life and growth, but as signs of madness and death" (Barnett 142). Clara, the main character of *A Movie Star Has to Star in Black and White*, suffers psychological fragmentation due to her pregnancy and subsequent miscarriage. Clara is a budding playwright, "trapped in a world in which her play production cannot compare in value to her reproduction" (Barnett 142). Also important to note is that Kennedy's characters most often become pregnant because of sociosexual oppression and/or rape. To become pregnant with another for these women means a splitting of their already fragmented self that leads to a further disintegration of their fragile being. The regret and hostility the characters feel towards the fetus is similar to the aggression that the female captive might feel towards her aggressor, but the tension created through such apparent psychical incarceration shows the female captive as emerging as more aware of possible ways of exploring her own needs and desires.

[3]McKay's article entitled "Reflections on Black Women Writers," published in 1987, gives significant historical background on various African American women writers who gave original voice to their experiences.

[4]Jean Fagan Yellin's article "Written by Herself: Harriet Jacobs' Slave Narrative" argues persuasively that Harriet Jacobs was indeed writing her autobiography with *Incidents*, and Yellin is credited both with raising this text to importance and with recognizing Jacobs as an important figure in African American literature. See co-editors Nellie Y. McKay and Frances Smith Foster's "Introduction" in the Norton Critical Edition of *Incidents in the Life of a Slave Girl* (Norton: New York, 2001) for a thorough discussion of the recovery of this text from obscurity.

[5]In her chapter entitled "Another Link to Life," Jacobs admits that upon learning that she had given birth to a baby girl, "[her] heart was heavier than it had ever been before. Slavery is terrible for men; but it is far more terrible for women. Superadded to the burden common to all, *they* have wrongs, and sufferings, and mortifications peculiarly their own" (64).

[6]Jacobs' decision to enter into a relationship with Mr. Sands derives out of a certain kindness that he extends to her and also out of an acceptance of the limited choices available to her. It is only after she is denied the simple right to marry whom she chooses (and she does chronicle her relationship with a free black man in "The Lover" to illustrate how free will was denied to even the "freest" of African Americans) that she makes the choice to move forward with what can only be viewed as a plan of survival.

[7] I speak specifically of the exclusion of pregnancy and childbirth in critical study. To be sure, the experience of motherhood has been of more interest to critics. Therefore, many of my secondary sources rely on the various discussions of motherhood for a passing comment about pregnancy and childbirth.

[8] Interviews can be found in *Conversations with Toni Morrison*, ed. Danille Taylor Guthrie (Jackson: University of Mississippi Press, 1994).

[9] Showalter likewise cites Alice Walker's groundbreaking teaching of courses on black women writers at Wellesley as well as other black feminist critics' "questioning the place of African American women within the literary canon as important steps in African American women discovering a political context that could include both race and class" (217).

[10] Interestingly, Morrison's Sethe is based upon a true account of a woman who did kill her children to save them from slavery.

CHAPTER 5

CAPTIVATED BY CAPTIVITY: HOW MEMOIRS REINSCRIBE PREGNANCY FOR THE CONTEMPORARY READER

> For the pregnant subject, pregnancy has a temporality of movement, growth, and change. The pregnant subject is not simply a splitting in which the two halves lie open and still, but a dialectic. The pregnant woman experiences herself as a source and participant in a creative process. —Iris Marion Young[1]

> A woman is never just pregnant nor just a mother.
> —Robin May Schott[2]

The works in this final chapter are privileged in a certain way because they emerge from a body of literature that has successfully inserted the pregnant and birthing body into popular and literary discourse. On the September 17, 2002, *Oprah* show, with Naomi Wolf as guest, several women found a forum to discuss the many "misconceptions" surrounding pregnancy, childbirth, nursing, and new motherhood. Many of the women featured on the show expressed how these experiences simultaneously "suck" and are some of the most enriching experiences of their lives. Though Wolf in her memoir/critical commentary *Misconceptions: Truth, Lies, and the Unexpected on the Journey to Motherhood* does not explicitly make reference to writers like Kate Chopin, Flannery O'Connor, or Toni Morrison, their presence is nonetheless discernible, most notably in Wolf's interrogation of the various accepted beliefs and practices that these writers consistently have called into question in their own works. The autonomy that women now have to celebrate and/or condemn their maternal bodies is put into question in Wolf's analysis, but what freedoms that women do have (limited or not) derive from the sacrifices of our foremothers and the strides made by certain women writers to bring these experiences to language. Recalling their desire that captivity might be reimagined into a kind of captivation with maternal bodies, with the incredible transformations that take place serving to challenge, compromise, and possibly to enrich a woman's understanding of herself in relation to the world, this chapter, with its concentration on the pregnancy memoir, shows an appreciation of all of that hard work.

This chapter also shows the dramatic leaps that have been made since Kate Chopin took the first huge step toward foregrounding and thus expressing the importance of the total experience of pregnancy, both negative and positive. This study concludes with a study of memoirs because such writings are the most likely to transform a woman's thinking about how her pregnant body affects both her understanding of herself and her interaction with the world at large through a reevaluation of the notion of captivity that pregnancy invokes. What these memoirs share is a poetic and philosophical approach to experiences that are usually treated with mundane practicality or disinterested dismissal. Here are women writers who have *chosen* pregnancy, women who are, in fact, free to choose in almost every aspect of their lives. Although Naomi Wolf's *Misconceptions*, Sandra Steingraber's *Having Faith: An Ecologist's Journey to Motherhood,* Louise Erdrich's *Blue Jay's Dance: A Birth Year*, and Carole Maso's *The Room Lit By Roses* are all quite different in the approach that each writer takes in recording her experiences of pregnancy and childbirth, a significant thread holding these memoirs together is a recognition of both the powerlessness and the hope that these experiences can inspire. Wolf, Steingraber, Erdrich, and Maso rewrite the "captivity" of pregnancy so as to make it a time of reflection, productivity, and monumental questioning. Most importantly, perhaps, is that they reinscribe the maternal body as a body worthy of reflection and philosophical attention. It is not a weak, passive, usurped body but rather a loaded, provocative, and eminently inspiring one.

Certainly the letters written to Margaret Sanger might be considered early, if unintentional, versions of the pregnancy memoir; these portrayals of pregnancy as the darkest of curses are indeed a far cry from the pregnancy journals that flood the Internet in the twenty-first century. While certain pregnancy e-journals might focus on the emotional highs and lows one experiences during pregnancy, essentially they lack studied thought on the philosophical ramifications of this experience. Still, the Internet is such an accessible and pervasive tool, it is necessary to investigate what pregnant women might find as they search for meaning and solace in cyberspace. Using key phrases like "philosophical impact of pregnancy" and "effect of pregnancy on women," and just simply "pregnancy and childbirth," reveal what a woman might find about pregnancy and childbirth on the web. On the positive side, if the pregnant subject or her partner desires to educate themselves on the biological stages of pregnancy, they will find just about all they need to know. In fact, certain websites like the Berkeley Parents Network include extensive subcategories that allow a woman to zero in on her exact situation. Pregnant with multiples? Dealing with the loss of a baby? Pregnant after 35? Questions about prenatal testing, leaking fluid, anal fissures? All of these queries are covered. However, what is perhaps disappointing is the fact that even the website originating from Berkeley, California—a place that holds nursing sit-ins and forwards women's rights in a number of ways—does not include a subsection on "philosophical impact of pregnancy" or anything remotely similar. The same cannot be said with regard to websites like <www.babyzone.com> where one must scroll through endless advertisements for diapers and maternity clothing to find anything of substance at all. While there are plenty of email postings charting individual women's pregnancies in sites like this, and there are sample "birth stories" that (too) succinctly sum up the experience, shockingly absent is any mention of the impact that these experiences have on women's psyches. There is little authorial restraint when dealing with the physical, whether it is a discussion of episiotomies or stretch marks, but there does seem to be a glaring erasure of what happens to a woman's mind as the baby takes center stage. Granted, many women's concerns are first and foremost with the physical state of the fetus, and worries regarding the proper nutrition, growth rate of baby, and fetal testing are indeed valid concerns, but where are the philosophical questionings, the fears of how this experience will change one's life and one's relationships?

Theoretical texts such as Julia Kristeva's "Women's Time" and Iris Marion Young's "Pregnant Embodiment" were in fact the first memoirs/ critical essays that I'd ever encountered that ventured beneath the surface to challenge my own understanding of the changes that I was going through in body and mind during pregnancy, but these two writers are not likely to penetrate the consciousness of the general public. Thankfully, with the emergence and proliferation of mothering blogs like Literarymama. com, women can connect with an effective moment-to-moment exploration of pregnancy and childbirth. American readers are also likely to run across Louise Erdrich's or Carole Maso's novels, and Naomi Wolf's and Sandra Steingraber's books were, thankfully, impossible to ignore given their authors' respective positions in the political limelight.

Although many readers felt that Naomi Wolf's *Misconceptions* charted new territory in its "revelations" about what she terms the "truth, lies, and the unexpected on the journey to motherhood," she herself acknowledges several works that paved the way for her own study. Wolf owes tremendous debt to various women writers who wrote of these issues long before she put pen to paper. Though not traditionally categorized as such, surely Adrienne Rich's *Of Woman Born*, referenced in the Introduction, includes one of the most famous examples of an "academic" pregnancy memoir. Her analysis of her own frustrations with pregnancy undoubtedly encouraged other women writers treated here, like Julia Kristeva, Iris Marion Young, and Robin May Schott, to explore their own experiences of pregnancy and childbirth as both interesting and worthy of scholarly attention. Rich was the first of these writers to exhibit reservations about pregnancy as philosophically transformative, but the pregnancy actually brings her out of a dark period when she was searching for a way to remake her life. She writes how she "had been trying to give birth to myself; and in some grim, dim way [she] was determined to use even pregnancy and parturition in that process" (29). While her pregnancy is not welcomed with unabashed joy, the fact of it does give her concentration enough to ground her in her own work. Rich decides to create out of difficulty, opting to "view our physicality as a resource, rather than a destiny" (39). Further, in her proclamation that "the child that I carry for nine months can be defined neither as me or as not-me" (64), Rich prepares us for the later works of Kristeva, a writer dedicated to highlighting the particularly evocative nature of pregnancy and the ways that it plays with distinctions with regard to body and mind. Rich's work, and by extension the works of those feminist theorists highlighted in the Introduction, is very important to the non-fiction memoirs of pregnancy that are discussed in this chapter perhaps because her memoir proves to be the most effective in challenging ideas about the pregnant and birthing body and thus revitalized the conversation about who ultimately "owns" these experiences.

Although Wolf does not explicitly name Rich as an inspiration, she does give credit to Jessica Mitford's popular and eyebrow-raising *The American Way of Birth* as a text that revived, in the late twentieth century, the painful and shameful stories of Sanger's hopeless throng of mothers, but Wolf also marvels at the fact that we have made very little progress since the 1992 publication of Mitford's book. Mitford apparently seeks to perform two functions with this book, debunking the many myths attached to pregnancy and childbirth in order to reinscribe these experiences within the women's sphere. She devotes a good deal of her treatise to assessing the past and the crude, oftentimes cruel, ways that women were treated during pregnancy and childbirth. In this assessment of past wrongs, Mitford hopes to set up a way of examining how an authoritative stance with regard to the birthing body is possible. Texts like Mitford's, which are too few and far between, have paved the way for writers like Wolf who believe that the conversation is far from over, and Wolf sees the need to take a different, more personal approach to the issues surrounding pregnancy and childbirth. Wolf references *The American Way of Birth* as one book that she reads upon finding herself pregnant, and she notes how both Mitford's text and Suzanne Arms' *Immaculate Deception* have failed to inspire the kind of reforms that pregnant and birthing women deserve. Wolf's "memoir," or so it might be categorized, is not as full of troubling and shocking statistics as is Mitford's; instead, she draws the reader into what is really a political treatise by engaging one in highly personal journeys of pregnancy, childbirth, and new motherhood.

In turn, Wolf's *Misconceptions,* published in 2001, is wholly engaging, completely accessible, disturbing, and fascinating to anyone who is contemplating or involved in pregnancy and childbirth. *Misconceptions* is certainly not the jargon-laded academic text that Wolf might have written; rather, she chooses to privilege the personal in grounding her analysis in her own experiences and those of various women with whom she interacts. In large measure, these are women who choose pregnancy, so they are by no means representative of the entire American population. In fact, since many of her featured women have delayed pregnancy and childbirth until their mid-to-late thirties or early forties, she spends a good deal of time examining the experiences of women who are not struggling financially. Rather, these are women often dealing with infertility, paying twenty thousand dollars a try in the attempt to become pregnant through in vitro fertilization. While she does focus primarily on the experiences of a rather elite group of women, this is perhaps not as serious a problem as one might imagine given the outcome of her study. In fact, it seems that even the women who comprise the "elite" are treated with condescension and a staggering lack of empathy by the medical establishment. The natural conclusion that any sensible reader might arrive at is to *really* worry how poor, lesser-educated women are treated. What Wolf finds particularly disturbing, and what she attempts to explain and amend, is the powerlessness she, a relatively powerful woman, feels inhabiting her own pregnant and birthing body.

Wolf argues on the first page of her book that during pregnancy and childbirth, "one of the most primal, joyful, lonely, sensual, psychological, challenging, and physically painful experiences she can face, [a women is] often overwhelmed by messages that infantilize who [she is] supposed to be, and mystify what is happening to [her]" (1). What prompts Wolf to write, apparently, is the great mystery of all that is pregnancy and childbirth. Indeed, I remember thinking when I was going through my twin pregnancy how incredible it was that I was actually housing three hearts, six kidneys, three brains, and the list goes on, and I recall a similar incredulity that no one seemed to share my belief in the *extraordinariness* of it all—that is, until I started reading what women writers had to say about it. We live in a culture in America that doesn't truly value the experiences of pregnancy and childbirth, and this fact can significantly compromise a woman's ability to be a voice of contradiction. However, Naomi Wolf, after the success of *The Beauty Myth*, has a sufficiently big or public voice to raise awareness of these issues, and her appearance on *Oprah* was one of the most widely watched and widely discussed talk shows ever. Of course, there was a good deal of backlash to both the show and the notion that there should ever be a negative comment made about pregnancy and childbirth, that it is "ungrateful" and "frivolous" to do so when one has healthy children as the outcome. Whether the reaction was overwhelmingly positive or negative is probably irrelevant. The fact is that millions of women are more informed about the realities of their pregnant and birthing bodies as a result of the publicity surrounding the publication of Wolf's book and the book itself. That her book is now often given at baby showers rather than a set of pink or blue booties is both important and interesting.

Wolf's work differs substantially from other "pregnancy handbooks" in its determination to look inward, as is shown in her realization of how she has been, quite literally, "invaded." As she looks at the ultrasound photo of her unborn child, she asks: "What was this new life—new life *form*? The weirdness was intense. Pearl, kernel, gem, nugget, faerie, night rider? There was someone in me; nurturing itself *from* me; what was the difference between this inner inhabitation and a kind of benign possession, or gentle succubus?" (30). Like most women, Wolf begins her own research with *What to Expect When You're Expecting* (Eisenberg and Murkoff), a book that she finally comes to think of as both comforting in its simplistic calming of fears and dangerous in the way that it steers women away from the questions that Wolf poses above. This so-called "pregnancy bible" tells Wolf to follow the "Best-odds diet," even though as a sensible person she wonders how it is possible to eat "five servings of bran or other unmodified grain product before nightfall" (24). She concludes that the writers vastly overstate the healthful foods a woman should consume so that she will at least consume some healthful ones because, she adds sarcastically, "we are too dumb, with only the facts presented to us, to moderate our intake like sensible bovines" (24). Indeed, it seems that the emphasis put on proper eating habits and *avoidance* habits during pregnancy is a way to divert the concerns that women should consider primary. And Wolf's tone does often reflect her anger at the way that pregnancy is packaged to women—as an experience in which women are asked only to "express ... a blossoming sense of joy and anticipation" (63). Like the early American women who write of their literal captivity, Wolf apparently believes that an inclusion of the darker, perhaps more negative qualities of experience (in her case, pregnancy and childbirth) can perhaps enhance the way that one absorbs and responds to such experience. To suppress the darkness, she argues, "actually mute[s] the experience of what [is] wonderful and affirming about it" (63). She also realizes that what she is feeling is an abundance of guilt, guilt for "not perpetually floating on air" (63). Of the women she speaks with, those who had better outcomes were the ones who felt they were prepared for pregnancy and childbirth both psychologically and physically. She quotes a Brazilian midwife who says that rather than minimizing the great pain of labor and delivery, women *should* candidly express the difficulty of it by revealing that women will have to become brave "warriors for themselves and their babies" (93).

While Wolf spends ample time questioning the medical establishment, she is centrally interested in the big questions that often lay low in the pregnant woman's consciousness, such as how exactly their intellectual, social, and sexual selves will change during and after pregnancy. Most notably, she asks the same questions that Tillie Olsen, Alice Walker, and, later Louise Erdrich, ask: What women in the past made real art or real revolution not only in spite of, but even because of, their lives with their children" (69). Further, Wolf writes of those notions that pregnant women shudder to think: "Where is the sexy mother, or the triumphant, battle-scarred mother, or the mother who is her own person while still being responsive to a child?" (68). Wolf also argues that "pregnant women and new mothers ... had few real role models to turn to" (68). Perhaps in writing this book she hopes to give us one. What she finds in her own pregnancy is anything but the ordinary. In fact, she finds herself confronting the politics of the medical establishment and how it affects pre- and post-natal care, she confronts body image and how pregnancy can disrupt one's self-image, and, finally, most interesting for the purposes of this dissertation, she evaluates how this experience forever alters her perceptions of herself as she relates to the world around her. She, like Mary Rowlandson before her, must emerge out of captivity to create herself anew, and in writing this "memoir," she is able to find a place to start in this new construction of self. Certainly there are times when she would like to return to her old self, to be able to "drink wine and smoke brown-black tobacco and flirt with strangers" (77), but the temptations of returning to that other self are transient. She ultimately realizes that she is dedicated to understanding and revealing the profundity of this experience. Wolf ventures into depths she never imagined, confronting her mortality in a most unlikely setting. In a swimming pool while on vacation, she feels the weight of her body and comes to a startling realization: "I felt as if I had slipped; I had fallen into a primordial soup of femaleness, of undifferentiated postfecundity. In my heightened state of anxiety, I felt myself standing on the slippery slope into aging and mortality, the universal slope I'd been able to ignore for so long" (77). With this fearful recognition of mortality, Wolf argues, "suddenly death seemed everywhere. It seemed to step lightly beside me during my pregnancy. Other women felt the same, but we somehow sensed we were not to discuss it" (78). A later conversation with a friend confirms these feelings of dread, when the friend explicitly states that "there are two times when you are completely alone. When you're pregnant. And when you die" (81). Still, Wolf finds solace, as the other writers I analyze here do, in honestly expressing her fears and apprehensions because these fears and apprehensions balance the desire of a "reconstituting of the self" (105) with the notion that "pregnancy ... like, perhaps, a terminal illness or a state of grace—seemed to make that barrier between the mundane, fretful, everyday world and the luminous 'ground of being' that much thinner" (105).

Susan Steingraber's *Having Faith*, in turn, is a curious pregnancy memoir in that it is part ecology/biology lesson and part personal journey. Steingraber's book is like Wolf's in its political agenda, and her approach is both didactic, in her eloquent delineation of how environmental hazards can threaten and disrupt the development of the fetus, and personal in the way that she, an ecologist, might locate a sense of power through the experience amidst these threats to herself and her baby. This study focuses on Part One of Steingraber's work, the section that depicts the unfolding events of fetal development. In this section, she offers nine chapters in which to frame her own pregnancy and names each after the month's full moon in the agricultural cycle. Steingraber's book is written the way a textbook *should* be written, as she manages to educate her reader about the intricate changes the pregnant body undergoes in such an engaging manner that we forget we are being taught. What she ultimately demands is collective attention to the rather phenomenal undertaking that is pregnancy, and she also explains how pregnancy has and continues to be threatened by a certain willful ignorance about and a short-sidedness to the many hidden dangers lurking in our everyday habitats.

Steingraber becomes pregnant at the age of thirty-eight, feeling "subtly hijacked" (32) by her new self. As an ecologist, she is amazed at how, to the outside world, nothing has changed with regard to her body or self, but on the inside, there is endless activity. With this observation, she launches into an analysis of the placenta, revealing that contrary to popular thought, it is not a barrier to toxic chemicals and pesticides. In fact, according to Steingraber, "chemicals don't even have to cross the placenta to cause harm" (34). At first glance, the reader might believe Steingraber's argument to be that mothers must be ever more vigilant about what goes in and around their bodies; actually, though, Steingraber asserts that this has been too much the case—placing the burden on the childbearing woman to abstain. In description after description of the toxic substances currently ignored by our government, she asks us to think of the ways that not only pregnant but all childbearing women are endangered. Thinking of getting pregnant? Then be sure to stay away from fish from ages 22-39 (because of the high mercury levels known to cause birth defects in some children—forget that fish contains much needed omega-3 fatty acids that aid in fetal development), move out of any house that you suspect has lead in the paint (but do we always know what lies beneath the latex?), do not drink tap water (or take showers, for that matter), and eat only organically-grown foods (which are increasingly expensive and simply unavailable to many). Steingraber experiences a profound sense of urgency in her first trimester over the ways that she and the world might make the environment more hospitable not only for her baby but for those of others as well.

Starting in Steingraber's second trimester, as is chronicled in "Egg Moon (April)," she notes how her hearing becomes increasingly sensitive. With the lethargic feeling of her first trimester behind her, she reveals how "torpor has given way to a state of high alertness" (58). It is in this same chapter that Steingraber details the events surrounding her amniocentesis, a test that can potentially reveal many different congenital problems. She explains, "Amniocentesis means puncturing a pregnant uterus and aspirating about 30 milliliters—one shot glass full—of amniotic fluid, which is then sent to a genetics lab for examination. The cells it contains are grown in tissue culture to increase their numbers and then inspected for chromosomal defects" (60). As a scientist, she recognizes the purported value of such a test, but she also wrestles with the implications of such knowledge, recognizing that "I now care so deeply about this pregnancy that I want to stop caring deeply until I get the results back" (61). She marvels at the way that handbook after handbook "allays" the fears of the mother undergoing a test that can potentially induce miscarriage by stating how "parents must weigh the potential value of the knowledge gained ... against the small risk of damaging what is in all probability a normal fetus" (61). Simple, succinct—no thought required, right? Wrong. Steingraber carefully details her own experience—the conflict over whether or not to have the test at all, her fear during and after the procedure, and then the interminable wait for the results—so that at least women in the same position will have an honest example from which to draw their own conclusions.

In "Mother's Moon (May)," Steingraber begins to contemplate the dramatic shift she is undergoing—from a person responsible only for herself to one busy housing, nourishing, and nurturing another. With the second trimester comes a sense of loneliness, a sense of isolation that extends to her relationships with her friends. Steingraber blames her solitary state, in part, on her friends' inability to recall and articulate what the second trimester is like, "although they are all too ready to discuss labor and delivery options" (94). During this time, Steingraber feels caught in a sort of limbo, likening her current state of pregnancy to "walking over a plank and cable bridge" with women who are not mothers on one side and a tribe of mothers on the other. She feels "neither here nor there...way up on the swaying bridge" (94). These philosophical questionings coincide with her need to feel the fetus moving inside of her, a sign of life and well-being usually detected between weeks sixteen and twenty. Frustrated at the minimal movement she is experiencing, and ever the scientist, she launches into a study of birth defects. Steingraber concludes that "there are reasons to suspect that environmental factors may contribute" (85) to certain birth defects like anencephaly, a neural tube defect which strikes early in development. Since about "95 percent of neural tube defects occur in families with no history of the disease" (85), she insists that our focus should be on environmental hazards. In particular, she notes, "we know the chances of anencephaly are greater among children of men whose occupations involve handling particular kinds of toxic chemicals" (85), like painters and pesticide applicators. Again, her personal history intersects with her scientific observations: first, as an adoptee, she has no family history records to confirm or deny a history of birth defects, and second, her husband, an artist by training, is also a painter who works with toxic substances. She reemphasizes that the burden is placed on her, the mother, to refashion actively her own environment in order to safeguard her child. So her husband quits his moonlighting painting jobs, and they move out of the apartment where lead paint is "sealed" behind new layers of latex, and, apparently, she sets out to write this book.

Perhaps given that she is a scientist herself, Steingraber does not vocally admonish the medical establishment in the way that Wolf does, but in her experience with childbirth education classes, she recognizes, as Wolf does, the culture of fear that is attached to labor and delivery. She describes her first childbirth education class as follows:

> We're a large group—there are twelve other couples—and a diverse one. Black, white, Latino, the age range is about twenty to forty. What unites the class—and separates Jeff and me from the rest—is fear. During the introductions, nearly every woman expresses how afraid she is of labor. One proclaims that all she wants to know is when she can get anesthesia. This brings nervous laughter all around. Another says, "I'm just really scared," and bursts into tears. This elicits sympathetic nods. The fathers-to-be don't have much to say for themselves, except that they are here to support their wives. They project a kind of blank awkwardness. Jeff and I exchange looks. Have we missed something? When it is my turn, I say as calmly as I can that I hope to have a natural childbirth. There is a moment of silence—no nodding of heads—and then the mother next to me clears her throat, states her first name, and says she has a really low tolerance for pain. (154)

In an attempt to counter what she interprets as possibly the other class members' ignorance of the stages of labor, Steingraber uses her chapter entitled "Green Corn Moon" to teach herself and her reader carefully about these important stages, in part to prepare her for her own journey but also because she seems compelled to educate given the glaring deficiencies in her own course. Steingraber's eager anticipation of the knowledge that such a course might provide quickly morphs into dread at the prospect of sitting through endless discussion of c-sections and episiotomies, with little or no time for discussion or the forging of "a supportive union of pregnant mothers who [might] embolden and encourage each other" (160). Further, while her instructor "does acknowledge that the surrender to drugs is not compulsory, she offers no alternative methods of pain relief other than just toughing it out" (161). Steingraber is frustrated and obviously angry at this omission because, as she sees it, "the choice is not between anesthesia and unremitting agony" (163). Rather, we might learn more about how natural childbirth attempts to "substitute nonpharmaceutical methods of alleviating pain" (163). In keeping with Steingraber's dedication to arming herself with as much knowledge as possible about the environment, she provides herself with the best company she can keep during her labor and delivery. She asks two women, one a retired midwife, the other an obstetrical nurse, to be there as "courageous presences" at the birth of her daughter. After she meets with these two women and discusses her desire for a drug-free childbirth, her husband asks if she is afraid. Steingraber responds, "Nope. I feel pretty brave" (176).

Early in her narrative, Steingraber argues that "no important journey ends without profoundly changing the one who undertakes it" (16). As a cancer survivor in her twenties, she endured inhabitation of the most negative of sorts as well as loss of control of her body but emerged more informed and powerful, and as a pregnant woman in her thirties, though dealing with a similar invasion of corporeal authority and feeling ill-equipped to take on the multiple dangers of her environment, she manages to emerge from these experiences with an equal sense of power. Steingraber's text not only provides countless readers with an interesting and accessible biological tutorial with regard to the pregnant and birthing body, but with the inclusion of her own narrative she highlights a grand pregnancy narrative that should be read and understood by everyone in America who claims to be interested in mothers and children.

Before Wolf and Steingraber, of course, there were others who recorded their perceptions of "confinement," like Harriet Jacobs or the women of Sanger's *Motherhood in Bondage*, but to writers like Erdrich and Maso, perhaps Adrienne Rich's brave exploration of her captive pregnant body was more likely a model for these writers' subsequent investigations. Louise Erdrich's study of pregnancy and childbirth is not limited to this single autobiographical work. In fact, her novel *Love Medicine* briefly references the ways that technology has affected the twentieth-century experience of pregnancy, and several of her other novels include birth stories. Critic Julie Tharp recognizes in Erdrich a dedication to highlighting the significance of birth stories as narratives that "connect an individual to other people in a web of family, community, or clan, functioning not so much as creation myths, but rather as connection myths" (127). Erdrich's *The Blue Jay's Dance: A Birth Year* is an autobiographical account of her own pregnancy and childbirth, and like Rich, she seems intent on viewing her pregnant body as a resource. Unlike Rich, however, she boldly explores the experience as destiny as well. She, like Wolf and a myriad of other women writers before her, asks how pregnancy and motherhood have affected the intellectual lives of women writers in the past. In fact, Erdrich provides lists much like Olsen does in *Silences*, carefully evaluating just who has made contributions to literary scholarship with or without being a mother. Like Alice Walker does in *In Search of Our Mother's Gardens*, Erdrich highlights the contributions of mothers, imagining "a wide and encompassing room filled with women lost in concentration," "absorbed in the creation of an emotional tapestry, an intellectual quilt" (145).

Erdrich's depiction of her own pregnancy in *The Blue Jay's Dance* is a far cry from the depictions we have in Sanger's work or in O'Connor's depiction of Ruby Hill. To be sure, Erdrich is in quite a different position than these other women; she has come to a place and time in her life when she is able to devote both the requisite energies and funds to welcoming a new life, and thus her attitude toward it is naturally more welcoming. That being said, Erdrich does have a profession in which she is thoroughly embedded. As a writer who must integrate this new experience into an already full and rich intellectual life, Erdrich uses this memoir to challenge both herself and the public to encourage and respect her pregnancy as a transformative and legitimate enterprise, as much a body of work as the text she is writing about it. Erdrich constructs the experience not as one in which she is held captive; rather, she is determined to write as one free to create this experience as independent of any fixed patterns. Ultimately, she transforms what might be passed off as the mundane into something redefining and revelatory, an experience that nourishes her both emotionally and intellectually.

In the first section entitled "Winter," Erdrich connects herself to those who have come before her, those who have chosen to tackle the life experiences of pregnancy, childbirth, and motherhood. Although Erdrich is writing as a respected and oft-anthologized author of late twentieth-century fiction, she identifies herself as one of those "many women [whose] work means necessary income" (5). She grounds this study in an important history of writing about pregnancy and childbirth that starts with Chopin, continues with broad strokes by Gilman and O'Connor, and culminates in an explosion of the genre in the last few decades of the century. Erdrich argues how as a writer, "work is emotional and intellectual survival: it is who I am" (5). Explicit in this quote and other moments scattered throughout Erdrich's memoir is a thoughtful evaluation of the philosophical impact of the decision to break with her intellectual life for a time in order to explore her body, the changes that pregnancy brings, and how she might bring the intellectual and the physical together. Erdrich has *chosen* this experience, and in that choice comes a certain luxury—the luxury to decide how this experience might enrich or empower rather than invade and corrupt. Nevertheless, many of the fears she expresses are the same fears that surface in earlier literature. O'Connor's Ruby Hill worries that she will never be "whole" again after she gives birth, and Erdrich similarly marvels at how the fetus inside her "is growing and dividing at such a rate I think I'll drop" (8). Like O'Connor's protagonist, Erdrich worries about possible loss of autonomy, but in her case it is a loss of the intellectual self when she realizes that in pregnancy she is "a physical self first," one woman among many who are "rounded vases of skin and bones and blood that seem impossibly engineered for birth" (9). At the same time, Erdrich echoes the words of Le Sueur's narrator in "The Annunciation" when she writes how she keeps herself in tune with her intellectual life by sustaining her writing: "On pharmacy prescription bags, dime-store notebooks, children's construction paper, I keep writing" (5). Writing for Erdrich, like the narrator of Le Sueur's story, allows her to conflate the experiences of pregnancy and childbirth with those experiences of the mind that she so values.

Erdrich does not lament her fecundity as Ruby Hill does; instead, she marvels at the miracle of how she can go about daily tasks while such monumental change is occurring in her body:

> I come here every day to work, starting while invisibly pregnant. I imagine myself somewhere else, into another skin, another person, another time. Yet simultaneously my body is constructing its own character. It requires no thought at all for me to form and fix a whole other person. First she is nothing, then she is growing and dividing at such a rate I think I'll drop. (8)

Her reflections on the seemingly impossible task of carrying a child to term reveal also a hesitation, a fear that her corporeal authority is to be challenged: "I can't figure out how I'll ever stretch wide enough. I fear I've made a ship inside a bottle. I'll have to break. I'm not me. I feel myself becoming less a person than a place, inhabited, a foreign land" (9). While Erdrich certainly is in awe of the changes her body undertakes, she senses a rupture of her own identity, and these concerns surely reference Julia Kristeva's argument about the splitting of the self that naturally occurs during pregnancy. In a succinct couple of pages Erdrich breaks with her narrative to comment on the many "chirpy and condescending" (11) instructions that are given to women with regard to pregnancy. She disparages the "pseudo-spiritual, misleading, silly, and even cruel" (11) advice that pervades pregnancy literature. Obviously, Erdrich responds with annoyance to American culture's infantilization of pregnant women, and the very writing of her own unique pregnancy narrative challenges the notion that pregnancy is but a predictable experience that can be reduced to one collective reading or interpretation. Erdrich's book is as unpredictable and thoughtful as the experiences of which she writes. It is alternately straightforward pregnancy memoir, recipe book, gardening manual, instructive text, and love letter to her husband and children. It is at the same time scattered and coherent. The breaks in her narrative serve to underscore the individuality of narratives of pregnancy and childbirth. Various sections are labeled as "Advice" or "Eating," strategically appropriating the terminology often used in the subsections of traditional pregnancy manuals, but hers is a far cry from any traditional manual, and she does her best to keep the reader on her toes. Her section entitled "Eating," for instance, is not a "best odds diet" like that found in *What to Expect When You're Expecting* (after all, she speaks of the comforting nature of a well-prepared frozen enchilada dinner) but, rather, reflects a fascination with the way that food has an effect on the growth of the fetus: "I never know which bite is destined for the heart, the muscles, hair, the bones forming like the stalks of flowers, or the lovely eyes" (13). In lighter moments, she offers the reader insights into what she deems the most "sensuous" foods to consume while pregnant: "a fresh cold cherry soup made with a little cream and cinnamon. Fry bread cooked small, in new oil, with a dollop of chokecherry jam. Hawaiian kettle-fried potato chips. Flan. Anything barbecued" (15). Erdrich is careful not to advise or encourage the pregnant woman to follow her practices, but clearly she views her text as necessary because she sees a dearth of realistic advice and narrative retelling.

With regard to the actual childbirth, Erdrich recognizes "the way to deal with [the] pain is not to call it something else but to increase in strength, to prepare the will" (12). By debunking many of the myths that various pregnancy manuals continue to engender, she can refashion the experience as an individual one in which women must recognize their determination by arguing that "women are strong, strong, terribly strong. We don't know how strong we are until we're pushing out our babies. We are too often treated like babies having babies when we should be in training, like acolytes, novices to high priesshood, like serious applicants for the space program" (12). In this paragraph, Erdrich aligns pregnancy with serious and challenging endeavors that should be met with reflection and respect. In fact, she reveals that her pregnancy and impending childbirth actually invigorates her creative writing, marveling at the energies she has to "write poems during the late nights up until the week of birth, and fiction by day" (24). Erdrich feels that she is "in touch with something larger than me," revealing with some surprise on her part that her work seems to be "hormone driven, inscribed in mother's milk, pregnant with itself" (24-5). In a section entitled "Hour of the Wolf," Erdrich again reveals a kindredness with Le Sueur's narrator in her belief that she is possessed in pregnancy with a certain creative force that might dissipate once she delivers her child: "I feel that I am transcribing verbatim from a flow of language running through the room, an ink current into which I dip the pen. It is a dark stream, swift running, a twisting flow that never doubles back" (25).

When Erdrich's narrative approaches the time when she will deliver, her section entitled "Famous Labors" explores her own vulnerability with regard to physical pain. "Why is no woman's labor as famous as the death of Socrates" (35), Erdrich asks, for surely any experience that involves the use of "basins and syringes and episiotomies" warrants our respect and admiration. Erdrich returns to the westernized culture's shameful dismissal of women's labor. She argues that "war heroes routinely receive medals for killing and defending. [So] why don't women routinely receive medals for giving birth?" (35). Erdrich's tale then moves to an acknowledgement of her own mother's labors, and she expresses a sense of wonderment at her mother's endurance of seven separate labors without drugs as well as her decision to breastfeed at a time when bottle-feeding was encouraged. Her appreciation for her mother's instincts transfers onto the midwife that Erdrich and her husband choose, a woman named Charlotte Houde who "tends to the entire existence of her patients" (37). Erdrich is aware that what she receives from her midwife is a kind of care that most women are never offered. Rather than glossing over the experiences of pregnancy and childbirth as some of the most positive experiences of a woman's life, this midwife tempers a hopeful attitude with a realistic understanding, providing Erdrich with a metaphor that serves her "during the blackest of moments" (37). Erdrich writes that Charlotte "compares the deepest wells of depression to gestation, to a time enclosed, a secluded lightlessness in which, unknown and unforced, we grow" (37). Erdrich holds on to these words as she prepares for "battle," recognizing her late pregnancy and subsequent labors as a time of captivity that precipitates captivation.

Erdrich next writes of her own labors in a section entitled "Women's Work," and perhaps surprisingly, she reveals a certain inability to articulate her experiences. Though she has endured two natural childbirths and one epidural-assisted childbirth, she finds "women's labor extremely difficult to describe" (42). She ponders this inability to bring the experience into language by noting that "perhaps there is no adequate description for something that happens with such full-on physical force" (43). But perhaps it is not that simple. Perhaps, Erdrich argues, it is the fact that we have been discouraged from articulating these experiences given that "women haven't had a voice or education, or have been overwhelmed, unconscious, stifled, just plain worn out or worse, ill to the death" (43). As a writer, she is frustrated by the fact that "birth is dictated to the consciousness by the conscious body" (43), and she is prevented from fully controlling the tale. As a writer, she finds this impossibly frustrating. Although she finds it difficult, Erdrich manages to articulate the "problem of the narrative," as she calls it, believing that it is not simply embarrassment about the physical that constrains the narrative but also a belittling of an experience that inhibits potential for real spiritual exploration. She writes that we are taught to devalue experience "in which we are bound up in the circular drama of human fate, in a state of heightened awareness and receptivity, at a crux where we intuit connections and, for a moment, unlock time's hold like a brace, even step from our bodies" (44). Do we tend to focus on the physical and limit the philosophical because we subconsciously fear what we might learn about ourselves if we were to give in to the philosophical questionings that pregnancy and birthing incite? Erdrich is a writer who is unafraid of asking the difficult questions, and as Tharp argues, she indicates in her writings, both autobiographical and fictional, "that pregnancy is a time of great power for women" (137).

Julie Tharp also notes that Louise Erdrich through her memoir and creative writing "joins an international group of women writers who are calling for a revaluation of maternal subjectivity" (139). Certainly Carole Maso should be included in such a group. Maso's memoir *The Room Lit By Roses* asks many of the same questions that Erdrich's does and follows along the same lines as Erdrich's memoir in its episodic nature and refusal to fit into a predetermined genre. With Erdrich's and Maso's reflective narratives, we can see the development of the pregnancy genre as it comes to us today. The only adherence to form is a shaky linearity that charts pregnancy from conception to post-partum time. Maso's journal-like writing is much more detailed than Erdrich's in its careful evaluation of the stages of reflection, fear, joy, and apprehension that she goes through as her body morphs into a visibly pregnant form. Given that Maso is both an older mother (past forty) and a lesbian, her memoir strikes out into largely uncharted territory. In writing this novel she writes herself out of another captive space—rejecting the notion that maternity is the province of the young, heterosexual woman. Her sexuality and her age become merely backdrops, however, for a careful consideration of how pregnancy intersects with several issues like academic pursuits, friendships, familial relationships, and independence. Not only does Maso provide a rich and comprehensive description of her own pregnancy, but she also includes within her narrative quotes from various writers who have informed her own reactions to her condition. Among these writers is Virginia Woolf, who was advised by her doctors not to have children due to her manic depressive nature. Maso suggests in quoting Woolf that she includes her among those who have aided her in her own explorations about the desire for pregnancy and motherhood.

Maso is more interested in a careful evaluation of her gestation rather than focusing more heavily on new motherhood. Further, she reveals the importance of separating these experiences by arguing that during gestation the baby is very abstract, that the pregnancy itself is somehow quite different from the actual experience of motherhood. Her memoir is one of the few that represents pregnancy as the slow maturation process that it is; further, Maso writes that "pregnancy is so mesmerizing" (69) that she wants to "prolong these feelings"(69). She does not jump from one month to the next; instead, she forces the reader to wait with her, oftentimes impatiently, as she reinforces the *slowness* of pregnancy, the sometimes torturous captive state of *waiting* that one must endure. Maso's communion with her pregnant self is enviable, and it becomes clear in reading of her experience that we have moved out of the realm of pregnancy as total impediment towards self-actualization. Nevertheless, Maso often reflects on how her perspective might have been altered had the pregnancy happened at an earlier date. Here we have a woman who has made a number of strides in her career; like Erdrich, she has earned a name for herself in academic circles. That this fact might alter how she views pregnancy at this stage in her life is not to be underestimated. Perhaps some might conclude that she is in too privileged a position to generalize about the philosophical possibilities inherent in pregnancy, but she speaks also as a marginalized female given her sexuality and advanced age. Maso also expresses her desperate desire to have this pregnancy come to fruition, and the greatest portion of the memoir focuses on the agonizingly vulnerable first trimester, when she is most likely to suffer a miscarriage.

Maso begins her memoir in a state of expectancy, unsure of the reality of the pregnancy, unsure of how to communicate this experience to the reader when she asks, "How to describe the blur of being pregnant?" (21). When she and her partner, Helen, finally confirm the pregnancy,

Maso realizes a sense of completeness: "I can scarcely believe what lives inside me—if only for this one moment. I look out at the transfigured universe" (6). As she begins to embrace this transformation that is taking place, she must reconcile her great joy at finding herself living an experience which she thought she might never have with the exhaustive pull of the first trimester—happiness tempered with a loss of control. Maso's narrative reveals the captive quality of pregnancy quite well in the inconsistencies with which she reads the experience, and in many ways she embraces and wholeheartedly accepts this captivity. Within a few lines she both exclaims at the fact that she "made two human feet today" (19) and laments "that a human being's birth dooms it to death" (19). Later in the text she is "astounded to imagine what magic a woman's body is capable of" (71), while on the next page she admits to missing her writing, insisting "nothing, not even [pregnancy] can take its place" (72). In many ways she describes the uncontrollable will of her body that she attempts to match with her intellectual evaluation of the experience. She finally accepts that the "pure violence of nature" is holding her captive to its will, that "the pure force, the drive to live—the desire to take shape" is "running riot in [her] body. It is part of the enormous exhaustion" (19). Maso describes this abnegation of control to be an odd mixture of "presence and absence," but ultimately she sees fit to reclaim control of the creation process that has begun in her body, finding herself "astounded in the end by my own resourcefulness" (20). Maso's descriptions of her experience follow along the same lines as Iris Marion Young's when Young explains how her own pregnancy "is most paradigmatic of such experience of being thrown into awareness of one's body" (165).

Even as she questions the compromised state of her pregnant body, Maso's memoir would definitely be categorized as a positive representation of pregnancy. Her inclusion of various apprehensive moments does not seek to subvert this aim; rather, her close communion with her body during pregnancy allows her the opportunity to question how this role will affect her productivity as a writer and, by extension, her intellectual self. She sees in pregnancy and her writing a similar opportunity for understanding of self, and she acknowledges her own fear that maternity might deny her certain opportunities of enrichment: "To hold the two simultaneously. To not deny either. Writing has taught me as much. An endeavor of utter discipline and utter playfulness. Rigor and recklessness. To control and relinquish control. Want. Dread. Resignation. Extraordinary hope" (21). This quote marks a triumph in many ways in the evolution of pregnancy narratives. Not only does this quote celebrate the fact that Maso and other women now have a choice with regard to pregnancy, but it likewise celebrates the creative mind of a woman as just as worthy of regard as the procreative body. Essentially Maso writes that her pregnancy has given her the same intellectual jolt that her writing has given her over the years, that it has the same ability to move her out of complacency into a place where she must experience moments during which a loss of control is necessary and perhaps productive. For Maso, pregnancy and writing stimulate both resignation and hope, and although she becomes in many ways a captive vessel and must relinquish control in pregnancy, she sees this captivity as a necessary component of intellectual growth. In fact, she is "intrigued by every single moment of this—even the frightening parts as they come," acknowledging that with every life experience "there is always some terror" (78).

Perhaps the works of Wolf, Steingraber, Erdrich, and Maso effectively close out this study of pregnancy as captivity because they so explode the term "captive" into one of multiple meanings, finally highlighting the most affirmative notion of all—that being captive to one's body during pregnancy and childbirth can prove to be one of the most provocative experiences of a woman's life. In achieving a definitive voice about women's experience, in giving legitimacy to the pains and pleasures of "captivity," these women take back the power to name these experiences as they see fit. Acknowledging the strength that characterizes these voices, we may begin to read pregnancy and childbirth as less a loss of authority and more of a promise of regeneration and renewal. Public perception has, in fact, been altered in various ways. The increased employment of experienced midwives and doulas, the availability of pre-natal exercise designed to strengthen body and mind, and the timely change in maternity wear to include styles that break the actual body out of captivity all evidence a dedication to revising the cultural script regarding these issues.

Naomi Wolf writes in *Misconceptions* that during pregnancy she "longed for something tangible that could reflect or give voice to those moments of otherworldliness [she] experienced. [She] wanted some acknowledgment of what [she] sometimes saw as the sacredness of [her] state" (103). Writers like Jacobs, Le Sueur, Olsen, Walker, Morrison, Steingraber, Erdrich, Maso, and Wolf herself have written these experiences, and in their beautiful, complex, devastating depictions, they have given us both the tangible evidence of the sacredness of pregnancy and childbirth and the strength to advocate the perpetuation of this important topic.

Notes

[1]From Young's "Pregnant Embodiment" in her collection entitled *Throwing Like a Girl and Other Essays*.
[2]From Schott's "Resurrecting Embodiment," p.178.

CONCLUSION

This project originated from an interest that I had in the discussions I was *not* engaging in about pregnancy and childbirth. My curiosity was peaked with one reading of Meridel Le Sueur's amazing "Annunciation," with the poetic vision that Le Sueur uses to transform a mere body into a repository of beauty and possibility. The project continued to challenge me as I searched for other writers who shared her interest in documenting these experiences. What I met with was a realization that we are afraid to approach the pregnant and birthing body, especially as feminists, as academics, who potentially have a lot to lose if we tie our inquiries women's history to the body. So the result is that many refuse to broach the topic at all. I found this absence of discussion disturbing, especially since I was contemplating pregnancy myself and wanted to consider it as more than a mere corporeal enterprise. Thankfully, I found others who seemed to share my incredulity, and buoyed by the knowledge of this, I sought to build upon those who have come to this topic before me.

It was in my own pregnancy—in the first trimester, in fact—that I started to think of the relevance of early American captivity narratives to my overall study of pregnancy and childbirth. These women were not pregnant while in captivity (though Hannah Dustan was just recovering from childbirth), but I nevertheless saw a number of similarities between the emotional and physical captivity endured by these women and the restraints put upon gestating women. Thus, these captivity narratives became useful examples of how one writes of an emotionally and physically restrictive experience, and they furthermore challenged me to reevaluate the term "captivity" as one with multiple meanings. Since this was a project dealing specifically with women's writing, it made sense to look back at some of the most widely read early writings of American women. Though Mary Rowlandson's and Mary Jemison's "captivity tales" were bestsellers, their readers were not exactly interested in them as evidence of female strength and endurance; rather, they were published with a nationalistic agenda to validate the continued subjugation and persecution of Native Americans. While that agenda was, sadly, the intended one, there is no doubt that in the past thirty or so years, these writings have been rediscovered for a different purpose—to give evidence to the fact that women were writing subversively even in early America when ostensibly they had little public voice. These women had penetrating voices and were quite varied in their responses to captivity. Rowlandson and Wakefield write of it as an instructive and life-altering experience; Dustan's account via Mather showed her as violently rebellious towards it; and Jemison chose to remain in captivity, embracing it. The recordings of these women, and their individualized reactions to restraint, I thought, paved the way for women writers who would later record experiences of pregnancy and childbirth. In essence, they created a blueprint for the pregnancy narrative as a version of the captivity narrative.

With the knowledge that these captivity narratives had proven useful in feminist studies in the late twentieth and twenty-first centuries, I decided to look at little known texts that included narratives of pregnancy, hoping to execute a similar rediscovery of contributions by women writers that had hitherto received little or no attention for their writing of pregnancy and childbirth. Kate Chopin's *The Awakening* is certainly widely read and studied, but I tried to read carefully the motivations and psychology of characters like Adèle Ratignolle and Doctor Mandelet in order to highlight the text's pregnancy narrative. I chose to argue that in including such narratives, writers like Chopin trigger a world of conversation that begins in the twentieth century with writers like Gilman, Wharton, and O'Connor and ends (at least for the purposes of this study) with writers like Wolf, Steingraber, Erdrich, and Maso.

My investigations of working-class writers like Le Sueur and Olsen dramatically altered my vision for this project when I realized the absolute commitment that these women had both publicly and privately to question and legitimate the experiences of pregnancy and motherhood. The representations of pregnancy in Le Sueur's "Annunciation" and Tillie Olsen's *Yonnondio* haunt the reader with visceral and often troubling images of pregnancy as it was experienced during the Great Depression. Yet both writers' take on pregnancy is that it must be individually written, and even in the midst of unimaginable destruction, pregnancy can promise definition and fulfillment as sure as it can promise debilitation and despair. In the beginning of my study of the works of African American writers, I was seeing in these pregnancy narratives *only* debilitation and despair, and until I truly began to understanding the reason for this, I was terribly frustrated with my need to prove that these narratives were hopeful with regard to the African American woman's experiencing pregnancy and childbirth. In the difficult months of writing this chapter, I came to realize that one does not necessarily dictate the direction of one's writing at all times. In fact, this chapter had me reevaluating my own understanding of pregnancy and childbirth—the fears, disappointments, and feelings of captivity (not captivation) that I had also experienced. Moving into the last chapter, I was met with these unsettling feelings again. Pregnant with my third child and re-reading Naomi Wolf's *Misconceptions* and Sandra Steingraber's *Having Faith*, I was confronted again with the dangers of carrying a child in an environment both literally and figuratively hostile towards the childbearing woman. These are not sunshiny documentations of the pregnant and birthing body, but neither are they, I realized, meant to induce panic. Rather, they are individual, informative, and honest depictions of a handful of women's experiences about what we *can* now claim is a philosophical and important journey.

This project has been for me an incredible educational *and* personal adventure. Given that many of the works that I study here are not even available on Amazon.com, I feel that one of my contributions has been to rescue works like *Yonnondio* and *Herland* from relative obscurity and to make certain that Flannery O'Connor's and Edith Wharton's lesser-known stories are not overlooked. I have also rediscovered the value and rewards of close, close reading. Furthermore, it has continuously amazed me the sincere interest that non-English majors have shown toward my study and the generous offerings of titles and recollections of pregnancy narratives that have continuously come my way. For this and many other reasons, I feel that this project has wider value and significant potential for reshaping American culture's vision of pregnancy and childbirth. And there is still much reshaping to be done. While this study ends on something of a hopeful note as to how we might reimagine pregnant and birthing bodies as captivating ones, the climate of fear in which we live and our ever-increasing dependence on technology bodes poorly for the kind of complete autonomy women should enjoy over their maternal bodies. As Tess Cosslett suggests in *Women Writing Childbirth*, the maternal body does indeed defy all cultural scripts and attempts to define and read it uniformly. The maternal body is an explosive one, literally and figuratively and stands ripe for more critical consideration. Perhaps further examinations of new forms of publication and dialogue and greater attention to factors such as age, ethnicity, class, and family composition will aid in our understanding of the ways that pregnancy and birth is being understood in American culture today. We are beginning to demand more transgressive readings of the pregnant body, as a fairly recent image in the November 2006 *Vanity Fair* would suggest. This photograph, of photographer Annie Leibowitz, aged 52, pregnant with her first child, is indeed transgressive. Leibowitz, an open lesbian and former partner of Susan Sontag (who took the photo before her death in 2004), defies all attempts to contain or inscribe the pregnant body with cultural and social tags. Leibowitz' pose recreates the infamous Demi Moore pose which Leibowitz shot in 1991. The tag line on the cover of the magazine simply reads "Annie Leibowitz does Demi Moore." The clever subtlety of the tagline evokes several responses, many of them potentially sexual. One could easily conclude that we will see photos of Demi Moore between the covers of the magazine, given that Leibowitz is most often the holder of the gaze. What we see, however, is both startling and exhilarating. Leibowitz is way past "advanced maternal age," she is a lesbian, and she is neither smiling or gazing up to the heavens. Leibowitz's photo is determinedly looking at the camera, a gaze that is most often her own, challenging the viewer to take it all in: her ample, sagging breasts with bulging, milk-filled veins; her abundant belly and ample thighs that have not been airbrushed to exclude cellulite. Her hair is shoulder-length but not exclusively feminine in appearance. In fact, the angularity of her face and the absence of make-up make her appear intensely androgynous. Most of all, she appears heroic; on first glance, I thought of the great warrior-women and goddesses. She suggests, with her defiance, that maternity is not to be simplistically represented or easily determined. The maternal body defies, explodes, and drastically alters the lives of those who choose to inhabit it. Her gaze is directly challenging those who might attempt to decipher or read her experience as anything other than one that is entirely her own. While the photograph is disappointingly placed far at the back of the magazine, the fact that it is there at all suggests the explosive possibilities for the inevitable freedom of the female captive maternal body. More, please.

BIBLIOGRAPHY

Albee, Edward. *Who's Afraid of Virginia Woolf?* New York: Penguin, 1983.

Arms, Suzanne. *Immaculate Deception*. New York: Bantam, 1977.

Bailey, Rebecca. "Clothes Encounters of the Gynelogical Kind: Medical Mandates and Maternity Modes in the USA, 1850-1990." *Dress and Gender: Making and Meaning in Cultural Contexts*. Eds. Ruth Barnes and Joanne B. Eicher. New York: St. Martin's, 1992.

Barnett, Claudia. "'This Fundamental Challenge to Identity': Reproduction and Representation in the Drama of Adrienne Kennedy." *Theatre Journal* 48.2 (1996): 141-155.

Bauer, Dale M. "Twilight Sleep: Edith Wharton's Brave New Politics." *Arizona Quarterly* 45.1 (1989): 49-71.

Baym, Nina. *Feminism and American Literary History*. New Jersey: Rutgers University Press, 1992.

Bendel-Simso, Mary. "Mothers, Women and Creole Mother-Women in Kate Chopin's South." *Southern Studies: An Interdisciplinary Journal of the South* 3.1 (1992): 37-44.

Betterton, Rosemary. "Prima Gravida: Reconfiguring the Maternal Body in Visual Representation." *Feminist Theory*. London: Sage, 2002.

Bordo, Susan. *Unbearable Weight: Feminism, Western Culture, and the Body*. Berkeley: University of California Press, 1993.

Bradstreet, Anne. "Before the Birth of One of Her Children." Ed. Nina Baym. *The Norton Anthology of American Literature*. Seventh Edition, Vol. B. New York: Norton, 2007. 205-206.

Bronte, Emily. *Wuthering Heights*. New York: Penguin, 1959.

Burke, Fielding. *Call Home the Heart: A Novel*. New York: Longmans, Green, and Co., 1932.

Burnham, Michelle. *Captivity and Sentiment: Cultural Exchange in American Literature, 1682-1861*. London: University Press of New England, 1997.

Burnham, Michelle. "Loopholes of Resistance: Harriet Jacobs' Slave Narrative and the Critique of Agency in Foucault." *Incidents in the Life of a Slave Girl*. Eds. Nellie Y. McKay and Frances Smith Foster. New York: Norton, 2001.

Butler, Judith. *Gender Trouble*. London: Routledge, 2006.

Carr, Karen L. "Optical Allusions: Hysterical Memories of and the Screening of Pregnant Sites." *Postmodern Culture* 5.2 (January 1995).

Case, Sue-Ellen. *Feminism and Theatre*. New York: Routledge, 1988.

Castiglia, Christopher. *Bound and Determined: Captivity, Culture-Crossing, and White Womanhood from Mary Rowlandson to Patty Hearst*. Chicago: University of Chicago Press, 1996.

Chopin, Kate. *The Awakening*. 1899. Ed. Margo Culley. New York: Norton, 1994.

Cixous, Hélène. "The Laugh of the Medusa." *Feminisms*. New Jersey: Rutgers University Press, 1997. 347-362.

Conboy, Katie, Nadia Medina, and Sarah Stanbury, eds. *Writing on the Body: Female Embodiment and Feminist Theory*. New York: Columbia University Press, 1997.

Cornell, Drucilla. *Feminism Beside Itself*. New York: Routledge, 1995.

Cosslett, Tess. *Women Writing Childbirth: Modern Discourses of Motherhood*. New York: Manchester University Press, 1994.

Daly, Brenda. "Seeds of Shame or Seeds of Change: When Daughters Give Birth to Their Father's Children." *This Giving Birth: Pregnancy and Childbirth in American Women's Writing*. Eds. Julie Tharp and Susan MacCallum. Bowling Green, OH: Bowling Green State University Popular Press, 2000.

de Beauvoir, Simone. *The Second Sex*. New York: Knopf, 1993.

Derounian-Stodola, Kathryn Zabelle. *Women's Indian Captivity Narratives*. New York: Penguin, 1998.

Eckard, Paula Gallant. *Maternal Body and Voice in Toni Morrison, Bobbie Ann Mason, and Lee Smith*. Columbia: University of Missouri Press.

Ehrenreich, Barbara and Dierdre English. *For Her Own Good*. Garden City, NY: Doubleday, 1978.

Eisenberg, Arlene and Heidi Murkoff. *What to Expect When You're Expecting*. New York: Workman Publishing, 1984.

Epstein, Julia. "The Pregnant Imagination, Women's Bodies, and Fetal Rights." *Inventing Maternity: Politics, Science, and Literature, 1650-1865*. Eds. Susan C. Greenfield and Carol Barash. Lexington: The University Press of Kentucky, 1999.

Erdrich, Louise. *The Blue Jay's Dance: A Birth Year*. New York: HarperPerennial, 1995.

Erdrich, Louise. *Love Medicine*. New York: HarperPerennial, 1984.

Faulkner, Mara. *Protest and Possibility in the Writing of Tillie Olsen*. Charlottesville: University of Virginia Press, 1993.

Firestone, Shulastone. *The Dialectic of Sex: The Case for a Feminist Revolution*. London: Women's Press, 1979.

Fishkin, Shelley Fisher. "Reading, Writing, and Arithmetic: The Lessons Silences Has Taught Us." *Silences*. New York: The Feminist Press, 2003.

Frankel, Haskel. "Review of *The Bluest Eye*." *New York Times Book Review* 1 (1970): 46-7.

Frye, Joanne. *Tillie Olsen: A Study of the Short Fiction*. Ann Arbor: University of Michigan Press, 1986.

Gelder, Ann. "Reforming the Body: 'Experience' and the Architecture of Imagination in Harriet Jacobs's *Incidents in the Life of a Slave Girl*." *Inventing Maternity: Politics, Science, and Literature, 1650-1865*. Eds. Susan C. Greenfield and Carol Barash. Lexington: The University Press of Kentucky, 1999.

Gilman, Charlotte Perkins. *Herland, The Yellow Wallpaper, and Selected Writings*. New York: Penguin, 1999.

Gilroy, Amanda. "'Candid Advice to the fair sex': or, the politics of maternity in late eighteenth-century Britain." *Body Matters: Feminism, Textuality, Corporeality*. Eds. Avril Horner and Angela Keane. Manchester: Manchester University Press, 2000. 17-28.

Gold, Michael. *Jews Without Money*. New York: Public Affairs, 2004.

Grosz, Elizabeth. *Volatile Bodies: Toward a Corporeal Feminism*. Bloomington: Indiana University Press, 1994.

Harris, Alice Kessler and Paul Lauter. "Introduction." *The Proletarian Moment*. Urbana: University of Illinois Press, 1991. i-xiii.

Hemingway, Ernest. "Indian Camp." *In Our Time*. New York: Simon & Schuster, 1925.

Herron, Carolivia. *Thereafter Johnnie*. New York: Random House, 1991.

Hurston, Zora Neale. *Their Eyes Were Watching God*. New York: Harper, 2006.

Irigaray, Luce. *Luce Irigaray: Key Writings*. Ed. Luce Irigaray. New York: Continuum, 2004.

Jacobs, Harriet. *Incidents in the Life of a Slave Girl*. New York: W.W. Norton, 2001.

James, Henry. *The Golden Bowl*. Oxford: Oxford World Classics, 1999.

James, Henry. *The Portrait of a Lady*. New York: Knopf, 1881.

Kahane, Claire. "The Maternal Legacy: The Grotesque Tradition in Flannery O'Connor's Female Gothic." *The Female Gothic*. Ed. Julian Fleenor. Montreal: Eden, 1983.

Kamel, Rose. "Literary Foremothers and Writers' Silences: Tillie Olsen's Autobiographical Fiction." *Contemporary American Women Writers*. Ed. Lois Parkinson Zamora. London and New York: Longman, 1998.

Kennedy, Adrienne. *Adrienne Kennedy in One Act*. Minneapolis: University of Minnesota Press, 1988.

Kennedy, Adrienne. *A Movie Star Has to Star in Black and White*

Kessler-Harris, Alice and Paul Lauter. "Introduction." *The Proletarian Moment*. James L. Murphy. Urbana: University of Illinois Press, 1991.

Ketler, Suzanne K. "Eating During Pregnancy: What's Good, What's Bad, Women's Ideas, and Representations in the Pregnancy Literature." *Crosscurrents* 7 (1995): 109-118.

Kolodny, Annette. *The Land Before Her: Fantasy and Experience of the American Frontiers, 1630-1860*. Chapel Hill: University of North Carolina Press, 1984.

Kristeva, Julia. "Motherhood According to Giovanni Bellini." *The Portable Kristeva*. Ed. Kelly Oliver. New York: Columbia University Press, 1997.

Kristeva, Julia. "Stabat Mater." *The Portable Kristeva*. Ed. Kelly Oliver. New York: Columbia University Press, 1997.

Kristeva, Julia. "Women's Time." *The Kristeva Reader*. Ed. Toril Moi. New York: Columbia University Press, 1986.

Lattin, Patricia Hopkins. "Childbirth and Motherhood in Kate Chopin's Fiction." *Regionalism and the Female Imagination* 4.1 (1978): 8-12.

Le Sueur, Meridel. *The Girl*. Cambridge, MA: West End Press, 1978.

Le Sueur, Meridel. *The Ripening: Selected Work, 1927-1980*. Old Westbury, New York: Feminist Press, 1982.

Lorde, Audre. "The Master's Tools Will Never Dismantle the Master's House." *Sister Outsider*. New York: The Crossing Press Feminist Series, 1984.

Lund, Michael. "Kate Chopin and Magazine Publication: Human Birth and Periodical Issue at the End of the Nineteenth Century." *Nineteenth Century Feminisms* 1 (1999) 95-117.

Madsen, Deborah L. *Feminist Theory and Literary Practice*. London: Pluto Press, 2000.

Maso, Carole. *The Room Lit by Roses: A Journal of Pregnancy and Birth*. Washington, D.C.: Counterpoint, 2000.

McKay, Nellie Y. "The Girls Who Became the Women: Childhood Memories in the Autobiographies of Harriet Jacobs, Mary Church Terrell, and Anne Moody." *Incidents in the Life of a Slave Girl*. Eds. Nellie Y. McKay and Frances Smith Foster. New York: Norton, 2001.

McKay, Nellie Y. and Frances Smith Foster, eds. *Incidents in the Life of a Slave Girl*. New York: Norton, 2001.

Michie, Helena. "Confinements: The Domestic in the Discourses of Upper-Middle-Class Pregnancy." *Feminisms*. Eds. Robyn R. Warhol and Diane Price Herndl. New Jersey: Rutgers University Press, 1997.

Mitford, Jessica. *The American Way of Birth*. London: Victor Gollancz, 1992.

Moi, Toril. *Sexual/Textual Politics*. London and New York: Routledge, 1985.

Morrison, Toni. *Beloved*. New York: Alfred A. Knopf, 1994.

Morrison, Toni. *The Bluest Eye*. New York: Plume, 1994.

Murphy, James L. *The Proletarian Moment*. Urbana: University of Illinois Press, 1991.

Namias, June. *White Captives: Gender and Ethnicity on the American Frontier*. Chapel Hill: University of North Carolina Press, 1993.

O'Connor, Flannery. "A Stroke of Good Fortune." *The Complete Stories*. Toronto: Doubleday, 1946.

O'Reilly, Andrea. "In Search of My Mother's Garden, I Found My Own: Mother-Love, Healing, and Identity in Toni Morrison's *Jazz*." *African American Review* 30.3 (1996): 367-79.

O'Reilly, Andrea. "Maternal Conceptions in Toni Morrison's *The Bluest Eye* and *Tar Baby*: 'A Woman has to be a Daughter Before She Can Be Any Kind of Woman.'" *This Giving Birth: Pregnancy and Childbirth in American Women's Writing*. Eds. Julie Tharp and Susan MacCallum. Bowling Green, OH: Bowling Green State University Popular Press, 2000.

Olsen, Tillie. *Silences*. New York: Delacorte Press, 1965.

Olsen, Tillie. *Yonnondio: From the Thirties*. New York: Delacorte Press, 1974.

Orr, Elaine Neil. *Subject to Negotiation: Reading Feminist Criticism and American Women's Fictions*. Charlottesville: University of Virginia Press, 1997.

Orr, Elaine Neil. *Tillie Olsen and a Feminist Spiritual Vision*. Oxford: University of Mississippi Press, 1987.

Pearlman, Mickey. Personal Interview. 1987.

Pearlman, Mickey and Abby H.P. Werlock. *Tillie Olsen*. Woodbridge, CT: Twayne Publishers, 1991.

Petchesky, Rosalind Pollack. "Foetal Images: the Power of Visual Culture in the Politics of Reproduction." *Reproductive Technologies: Gender, Motherhood and Medicine.* Ed. Michele Stanworth. Minneapolis: University of Minnesota Press, 1987.

Pratt, Linda Ray. "Woman Writer in the CP: The Case of Meridel Le Sueur." *Women's Studies* 14 (1988): 247-264.

Rabinowitz, Paula. "Maternity as History: Gender and the Transformation of Genre in Meridel Le Sueur's *The Girl.*" *Contemporary Literature* 29.4 (1988): 538-548.

Rich, Adrienne. *Of Woman Born: Motherhood as Experience and Institution.* New York: Norton, 1976.

Roberts, Nora Ruth. *Three Radical Women Writers: Class and Gender in Meridel LeSueur, Tillie Olsen, and Josephine Herbst.* London: Routledge, 1996.

Rogers, Deborah D. "Rockabye Lady: Pregnancy as Punishment in Popular Culture." *Journal of American Studies* 26.1 (1992): 81-83.

Sagre, Gordon M. *American Captivity Narratives.* Boston: Houghton Mifflin, 2000.

Sanger, Margaret. *Motherhood in Bondage.* Columbus: Ohio State University Press, 2000.

Sapphire. *Push.* New York: Knopf, 1996.

Saul, Jennifer Mather. *Feminism: Issues and Arguments.* Oxford: Oxford University Press, 2004.

Schott, Robin May. "Resurrecting Embodiment: Toward a Feminist Materialism." *A Mind of One's Own: Feminist Essays on Reason and Objectivity.* Eds. Louise M. Antony and Charlotte Witt. Boulder: Westview Press, 1993.

Schweitzer, Ivy. "Maternal Discourse and the Romance of Self-Possession in Kate Chopin's *The Awakening.*" *Boundary 2: An International Journal of Literature and Culture* 17.1 (1990): 158-86.

Shange, Ntosake. *Spell #7.* New York: French, 1981.

Showalter, Elaine. *A Literature of Their Own.* Princeton, NJ: Princeton University Press, 1977.

Skaggs, Peggy. *Kate Chopin.* Boston: Twayne, 1985.

Slesinger, Tess. *The Unpossessed: A Novel of the Thirties.* New York: NYRB Classics, 2002.

Smith, Valerie. "Form and Ideology in Three Slave Narratives. *Incidents in the Life of a Slave Girl.* Eds. Nellie Y. McKay and Frances Smith Foster. New York: Norton, 2001.

Spivak, Gayatri Chakravorty. *The Spivak Reader.* Ed. Donna Landry and Gerald MacLean. New York: Routledge, 1996.

Staub, Michael. "The Struggle for 'Selfness' Through Speech in Olsen's

Yonnondio: From the Thirties." *Studies in American Fiction* 4 (1999) 131-135.

Steingraber, Sandra. *Having Faith: An Ecologist's Journey to Motherhood*. Cambridge, Mass: Perseus, 2001.

Tarter, Michele Lise. "Bringing Forth Life from Body to Text: The Reclamation of Childbirth in Women's Literature." *This Giving Birth: Pregnancy and Childbirth in American Women's Writing*. Eds. Julie Tharp and Susan MacCallum. Bowling Green, OH: Bowling Green State University Popular Press, 2000.

Taves, Ann. "Spiritual Purity and Sexual Shame: Religious Themes in the Writings of Harriet Jacobs." *Incidents in the Life of a Slave Girl*. Eds. Nellie Y. McKay and Frances Smith Foster. New York: Norton, 2001.

Tharp, Julie. "'Into the Birth House' With Louise Erdrich." *This Giving Birth: Pregnancy and Childbirth in American Women's Writing*. Eds. Julie Tharp and Susan MacCallum. Bowling Green, OH: Bowling Green State University Popular Press, 2000.

Tharp, Julie and Susan MacCallum Whitcomb. *This Giving Birth: Pregnancy and Childbirth in American Women's Writing*. Bowling Green, OH: Bowling Green State University Popular Press, 2000.

Wade-Gayles, Gloria. "The Truths of Our Mothers' Lives: Mother-Daughter Relationships in Black Women's Fiction." *SAGE: A Scholarly Journal on Black Women* 1.2 (1984): 8-12.

Walker, Alice. *The Color Purple*. New York: Harcourt Brace Jovanovich, 1992.

Walker, Alice. *In Search of Our Mother's Gardens*. New York: Harcourt Brace Jovanovich, 1983.

Walker, Alice. *Meridian*. New York: Harcourt Brace Jovanovich, 1976.

Wharton, Edith. *Twilight Sleep*. New York: Scribner, 1927.

White, Deborah Gray. *Ar'n't I a Woman? Female Slaves in the Plantation South*. New York: Norton, 1999.

Williams, Tennessee. *A Streetcar Named Desire*. New York: New Directions, 1947.

Wittig, Monique. *The Straight Mind and Other Essays*. Boston: Beacon Press, 1992.

Wolf, Naomi. *Misconceptions: Truth, Lies, and the Unexpected on the Journey to Motherhood*. New York: Doubleday, 2002.

Wolf, Naomi. *The Beauty Myth*. New York: William Morrow and Co., 1991.

Wollstonecraft, Mary. *A Vindication of the Rights of Women: With Strictures on Political and Moral Subjects*. New York: Norton and